Through the Fog

A volume in
Urban Education Studies Series
Nicholas Daniel Hartlep, Thandeka K. Chapman, and Kenny Varner *Series Editors*

Through the Fog

Towards Inclusive Anti-Racist Teaching

Tara L. Affolter

Middlebury College

INFORMATION AGE PUBLISHING, INC.
Charlotte, NC • www.infoagepub.com

Library of Congress Cataloging-in-Publication Data

Names: Affolter, Tara L., author.
Title: Through the fog : towards inclusive anti-racist teaching / Tara L.
  Affolter.
Description: Charlotte, NC : Information Age Publishing, Inc., 2019. |
  Series: Urban education series | Includes bibliographical references. |
  Identifiers: LCCN 2018052151 (print) | LCCN 2019005512 (ebook) | ISBN
  9781641134798 (Ebook) | ISBN 9781641134781 (harcover) | ISBN
9781641134774
  (pbk.)
Subjects: LCSH: Racism in education–United States. | Discrimination in
  education–United States. | Educational equalization–United States. |
  Minorities–Education–United States. | Teachers–United
States–Attitudes.
Classification: LCC LC212.2 (ebook) | LCC LC212.2 .A54 2019 (print) | DDC
  379.2/6–dc23
LC record available at https://lccn.loc.gov/2018052151

Cover Art: Jerry L. Hoffman, 2018

. . . you kind of learn how to navigate. It is almost like when I drive in on a Monday morning and there is fog on the highway, I know that if I am careful I will get there. But, if I am driving fast through the fog, I could hit a deer . . . all kinds of things. I kind of feel that in terms of working with people in my department, it is like that Monday morning fog and just be careful, you will get there, even without them, you will get there.

—Ms. Wilson, teacher

Contents

Prologue

Janie stood where he left her for unmeasured time and thought. She stood there until something fell off the shelf inside her. Then she went inside there to see what it was. It was her image of Jody tumbled down and shattered. But looking at it she saw it was never the flesh and blood figure of her dreams. Just something she had grabbed up to drape her dreams over.

—*Their Eyes Were Watching God*, Zora Neale Hurston (1990)

November 13, 2016

It's Sunday morning. Almost a week ago my country elected a president that represents the very worst of itself. Correction: white people elected a president that reflects the very worst of them (our)selves. White women chose white supremacy over all else. As a white woman I am beyond ashamed. As a United States citizen, I am horrified of what this means for our country. (And since the time of this entry we have seen in visceral terms, in marches, political rallies, and policy decisions what overt white supremacy looks like.) White women looked past even their own self-interests to vote for a man and cement the power of a party that promotes xenophobia, nationalism, white supremacy, ableism, sexism, homophobia, transphobia, and racism, racism, racism in so many forms it's hard to find the right label for it. I am a white woman and the parent of an African American child (now an adult). I am terrified by the white lash that has been released with the election of this president. This is not a new story for this country or a new fear, but it is heightened for me at least.

In the wake of the election I have raged, cried, and protested. I dreamt my African American son was being hunted through the woods; the hunter's faces obscured but their white skin glowing. I have reached out to some people and have avoided others. I held a listening circle in which a Latinx student broke down over fear for her family and the rest of the class gave her space to grieve. I have had students hang on to me for long hugs and others just ask if they can sit in my office for awhile. I have confronted the dangerous parts of myself that want to scream in the face of the white college student who takes a seat in the front row smirking and singing as he wanders into class 2 days after the election with a Trump sticker affixed to his computer. His smirk says, "Now what about your desire for equity?" The same student will later tell the class that "we need to redefine what inclusion means, because it probably is just for citizens" and under this administration inclusion means that "illegals" can't be part of our schools.

I have rejected the messages that have filled my in-box and Facebook feed, calling for unity. I have avoided campus gatherings that allow "both sides to voice their feelings." Anti-racist inclusion does not have room for hearing about how it is okay to hate people of color and espouse white supremacy. I have resisted pretending that things are normal. I have yelled at meetings, sworn at inappropriate times, woken in the middle of the night, and put on pajamas and crawled into bed in the middle of the afternoon. None of this helps.

And in all of this nothing has to do with the grief and disbelief that is bubbling underneath. My image of what I thought the United States could be, not what was, but in the hope of what it could be and the belief people would ultimately work towards that vision, fell off the shelf and shattered. But why? How can I, a woman heavily influenced by critical race theory, be really shocked that white supremacy won again? This isn't a change, but a predictable map that has played out again and again. And yet I am shocked. And embarrassed by the shock. I realize that despite my attempts to engage critically with race I too had been lulled into a false sense of comfort and security thinking white supremacy could not win—a security that comes from being white and thinking we as a nation were beyond such overt racism. I am implicated in a skit on Saturday Night Live that Saturday after the election in which Dave Chappell and Chris Rock mocked their liberal white friends in their exaggerated devastation over Trump winning. At one point, one of the white characters says, "This is the worst thing this country has ever done." Chappell and Rock, both African American men, exchange knowing looks and explode into laughter as whites once again forget the brutal history of the United States. I am angry at the 52% of white woman who voted for Trump. I find myself wondering about other whites (Did you do this?). I am frustrated with those that played nice or tried to be neutral, am frustrated with myself for believing that this nation had begun to move forward, however incrementally, in its progress towards equity and racial justice.

Briefly after the election there was a movement (on Facebook at least) for white allies to wear safety pins to identify themselves as such. While I understand the sentiment and the desire to pin oneself as a good white person—the action seems too facile. Once again whites can slip (or in this case) clip on a symbol of anti-oppression, wear it so others can see they are good, go home to white enclaves, unclip, and sleep the sleep of those who have not grappled with the pain of fearing for their lives. (I wonder why the safety pin call wasn't for something more overt—what about, for example, attaching a Black Lives Matter button to that empty safety pin?) I was disillusioned enough with the safety pin movement to post about the problems with it on Facebook. I received a fair amount of backlash from white friends telling me I shouldn't paint all whites with the same brush. I was reminded by them that I was white too and shouldn't forget that and maybe I should try kindness. Maybe I should accept good will gestures and not be so jaded—after all I am white and I should understand these gestures and the ultimate good will undergirding them. Right? I don't feel kind and I don't feel like working from a place of love and I don't trust the "good will" of whites. This makes me sad, and it is a slippery slope as a white person working to be less of an ally and more of an accomplice to disassociate myself with other white people. But, I think something inside me had to be shattered to continue this work.

All of this brings me to this book, which I started years ago, speaking to why we need inclusive anti-racist classrooms: a book that stalled as I faced numerous health and family crises; a book that was rejected by some as too personal or too confrontational and others as a literary version of a safety pin. The book comes from years of research and practice that I have positioned under the banner of anti-racist—research that at times has been rejected because of the very use of the term anti-racist—either too political or too dated. And yet here we are again and the need for overt and dedicated anti-racist practice has never been clearer.

I don't know where to go from here. I know that of the 52% of white women who voted for Trump, at least some of them are teachers. They teach the very children that a xenophobic, ableist, sexist, and white supremacist government want to erase. They send messages that we must respect the rule of law, even when such a law puts into question a child and her family's very existence in this county. And they teach the white young men and women that are forming the backbone of the ever-strengthening alt-right, white supremacist movement in this country.

Following the election of the 45th president, the Southern Poverty Law Center has reported a significant increase in hate crimes and harassment. The majority of these acts are taking place in K–12 schools. Clearly teachers have work to do. Suggesting "neutrality" in the classroom, or thinking what one does and the policies one supports has no bearing in the classroom is a dangerous myth with dire consequences. Any question of this danger in neutrality was spelled out in August of 2017 when the 45th president blamed "both sides" for a white supremacist rally that ended in the murder of an anti-racist protestor and the injury of many more anti-racist activists.

I know that if we are to ever move away from racist practices and policies, whites must change. I know if we are ever to achieve a just and compassionate world, we must look at the ways we allow ableism to run rampant and some people (those with atypical bodies for example) to be excluded from a definition of inclusion. So, let's begin.

Introduction

We are citizens of a country that we still have to create—a just country, a compassionate country, a forgiving country, a multiracial, multireligious country, a joyful country that cares about its children and about its elders, that cares about itself and about the world, that cares about what the earth needs as well as what individual people need.

—Vincent Harding, speaking at the Children's Defense Fund, National and Racial Healing Town Hall, July 2012

In 2013, the summer I began this book, George Zimmerman was acquitted for the murder of Trayvon Martin, an unarmed Black teen who made the "mistake" of taking a shortcut through Zimmerman's neighborhood while wearing a hooded sweatshirt. When Trayvon was murdered I remember staring at his picture and thinking of how young he was and how easily that could have been my son. I am white. My son is Black and just a few years older than Trayvon. I spoke to white family members about my fears of losing my son to state sanctioned violence and one stated, "Yes, I know having teenagers will make you crazy." This was spoken as if the perils I was speaking of had to do with the zany antics of youth and not the systemic targeting of Black bodies.

I spoke to African American friends and mothers and the reaction was quite different. One close friend told me, "We are parents of an endangered

Through the Fog, pages xv–xxvi
Copyright © 2019 by Information Age Publishing
All rights of reproduction in any form reserved.

species . . . they lock them up, or shoot them down. I am holding on to my baby tight." But we both knew that no amount of clutching our children closer could ultimately protect them from the racism that shapes the world.

Following the murder of Trayvon Martin, President Obama made the remark, "If I had a son, he would look like Trayvon." Pundits pounced on this remark critiquing the president for "making this about race." I read this and wanted to scream. It was about race long before President Obama's comments and it continues to be about race. Again, and again, the news distorts and oversimplifies the issues and paints one-dimensional and often damaging pictures of those who are victims of police murder and other forms of state sanctioned racism.

In the follow-up coverage to Michael Brown's murder by a white police officer, in Ferguson, Missouri, Brown was portrayed as either a college bound youth or a dangerous criminal. Somewhere in there, we lost what many in classrooms around the country already know—Michael Brown, Trayvon Martin, Sandra Bland, Oscar Grant, Reika Boyd, Shelly Fay, Tamir Rice, Freddie Gray, and the many young Black men and women that were taken too soon are young people attempting to live and learn in a world that seeks to belittle them and cast their lives in a deficit and nullifying narrative. They are a part of our communities and our families and our schools. They are neither thugs nor saints, but young people trying to learn, grow, challenge, and above all, *live* in a world that often attempts to erase them. We don't need to highlight Michael Brown's virtues or deficits. We don't need to be told that Jordan Edwards was an honor student and not a thug so his life mattered more. What we need to realize is that BLACK LIVES MATTER. Our children, *all of our children*, deserve high quality education in which they can be seen, cherished, and valued for their unique gifts and human foibles.

To some this may seem obvious, yet we have a society in which our Black and Brown children can be suspended, expelled, locked up, and murdered, and somehow it isn't a national emergency. Somehow white America can remove itself from the fray. We are in a country in which white men and women appear on television and around dinner tables scolding "those" people for protesting and sadly shaking heads at a loss of supposed decorum (and niceness). We see heated defenses of a white school police officer when he accosts a 15-year-old Black girl; toppling the desk she is in to the ground and then dragging her to the front of a room of classmates. Her offense was simply a refusal to give up her cell phone. Who gets to be a teenager in this country? Who gets to be a child? Dealing with students that break rules is part of the territory for educators. It shouldn't result in bodily harm and public shame.

And then there is Charleston, South Carolina. I still reel from the murders of nine African Americans at Mother Emmanuel Church. This terrorist attack is not an isolated incident. It is to be sure, horrifying in its scale and in the overt racial hatred that spawned the attack. And even then, there was denial by some in the media, claiming the attack was religious based and not racial, even though the killer specifically stated racist reasons for his attack! As I enter revisions for this project I have added more names to the list of those murdered, fumed as a white college aged rapist was given a light sentence, read about another Black man killed for following the directions of a police officer, and another killed for having a cell phone in his grandmother's backyard. I've witnessed the media-shaming cries for criminal charges to be brought against a Black mother when her toddler slipped through the bars of a gorilla cage and the gorilla was killed in order to save the child. A few weeks later, a white toddler was killed by an alligator when he was wading near the edge of a pond where signs were posted to "stay out of the water." The names of those parents did not become public fodder for shame and ridicule. No public outcry followed, no searching the criminal history of the parents, or calling for criminal charges. The examples of white supremacy pile up as the racism in this country thickens again, reforms, and wraps in a new way around our country.

We now have a white supremacist holding the office of president who defends Nazis and fellow white supremacists and earns praise from Klan members and other alt-right fascists. As I work on final page proofs of this book many of us are still reeling from the shooting rampage at the Tree of Life Synagogue in Pittsburg that left 11 people dead. The killer had allegedly been incensed by this congregations sheltering and care of immigrants and refugees. The nation's president has spent the last several week's inciting racial fear and hatred towards refugees seeking asylum in the United States.

Whites around the country insist on false notions of "free speech" and offer tepid defamation of white supremacy in all forms. By the time this book is completed there will be more racist attacks, big and small. Some will be noted on the news, most will go unremarked upon locally and nationally. All will do damage.

I have two reactions when I see the faces of perpetrators and victims of racial terrorism. First, in the faces of the victims I see my students, my friends, and my family. I remember staring at the picture of Tamir Rice, the 12-year-old boy that was gunned down by a police officer in Cleveland, Ohio. I recognized his goofy smile. The picture I see most often is one in which he appears to be at a diner, grinning without showing any teeth. Perhaps he just had his favorite milkshake or was trying to charm a dinner companion into ordering him some dessert. His face is that of a boy, because that is what he was, *a child.* In the background, a white patron is caught staring in the direction of the camera, staring at Tamir, wearing either a blank or menacing expression. Regardless of the interpretation, the gaze at this Black child from a white stranger haunts me.

I am also reminded of the ways white women in particular have been anything but "nice," in their support of white supremacy. I will talk more throughout the text about white women and our involvement in sustaining whiteness, but for now consider another photograph. There is a famous image of Elizabeth Eckford, a young Black girl who was part of the Little Rock Nine. In it, Elizabeth walks alone toward Little Rock High School (she wears a dress she made herself for the special occasion). She is followed by a trio of white women (one of them a high school student herself). The trio sneers at Eckford. Their mouths are contorted with the taunts they rain down on her—their faces frozen masks of hate. I see Elizabeth, a young Black girl, clutching her books to her chest, walking head up and staring straight ahead. She is alone and she is still a child, and yet none of this matters.

These photos haunt me. I am fearful of all the ways white people have perpetrated damage and how we have made it criminal to simply be a Black child in America. I am ashamed of the legacy of white women in this reality. And I am reminded of the many ways that we have failed all of our students in the education system by not dismantling systemic racism. Since white women continue to make up the bulk of our teaching force, we cannot hide from our cosigning the replication of white supremacy.

This book is an attempt to continue to encourage educators to see all of our students in this struggle and not replicate the kind of teaching that allows a Black youth in a hoodie to be seen as a threat simply in his existence. It is an attempt to disrupt the narrative in which a white student can go to a racially diverse school and still see him or herself as superior and more deserving. Or a white student can attend an all-white school and decide that race is something for "other" people. It is an attempt to support white teachers as they sort through their own racialized socialization. In the end, it is neither a pretty or tidy story. And no, "nice white ladies" are not saviors of Black and Brown communities. We are, however, responsible for the way that white supremacy has infected our teaching, our curricula, our policies, our practices, and our lives. Black and Brown communities don't need white folks to explain racism to them. White folks need to do the work to end this systemic and deliberate perpetuation of white supremacy.

The rhetoric around public education attempts to obscure this truth and works to avoid implicating whiteness. This is particularly true in the destruction and lack of support for urban schools. There is a steady refrain in reference to urban education one that declares: failing students, failing teachers, school-to-prison-pipeline, "minority" student achievement gap, *those* parents, *those* kids, *those* neighborhoods. High stakes tests replace quality curricula and stand in for thoughtful educational policy. Students and in urban public schools have become the testing group for white-led educational reform in the form of "no excuse" charters in which students are subjected to some of the most limited curricula and practices. Mass school closures are taking place in urban centers across the country, and in the steady march of privatizing schools, we are losing sight of the potential for equitable education for all. These policies, practices, and procedures, from high stakes testing to school closures, have a disproportionately negative impact on urban schools serving large communities of color.

Lost in these policy decisions, swallowed in this media coverage, and ignored in this move to "reform" schools, are the teachers, students, parents, and community members who comprise urban public schools. For example, in Chicago where Black students made up 40% of the public-school population in 2013 they made up 88% of the students whose schools were closed. Yet, 87.5% of those students were sent to schools that were not significantly higher performing and to teachers that were unprepared and unsupported for the influx of new students into their schools (Cohen, 2016). These patterns are repeated in urban centers across the country with the most striking example in post-Katrina New Orleans where there no longer exist any traditional public schools and the large African American teaching force that existed prior to Hurricane Katrina was decimated by mass firing at the state level (Henry, 2016). A majority of these teachers were replaced by white teachers with much less experience and less training and little connection to the communities in which they were recruited to teach.

One of the most extensive examples of the inequities faced by students of color in our schools comes from the 2013–2014 Civil Rights Data Collection (CDRC). The CRDC is a survey of all public schools and districts in the United States. Data collected "measures student access to courses, programs, instructional and other staff and resources—as well as school climate factors such as student discipline and bullying and harassment—that impact education, equity and opportunity for students" (U.S. Department of Education Office of Civil Rights, 2016, p. 1). The "First Look" report of this data reveals the students of color face vastly different treatment than their white peers in schools across the nation. For example,

▪ Black preschool children are 3.6 times as likely to be suspended than white preschool students.

- Black K–12 students are 3.8 times as likely to receive one or more out-of-school suspensions as white students.
- Black girls are 8% of enrolled students, but 13% of students receiving one or more out-of-school suspensions. Girls of other races did not disproportionately receive one or more out-of-school suspensions.
- American Indian or Alaska Native, Latino, Native Hawaiian, or other Pacific Islander, and multiracial boys are also disproportionately suspended from school, representing 15% of K–12 students but 19% of K–12 students receiving one or more out-of-school suspensions. (pp. 2–3)

Further, the press release highlighting this study clearly shows urban areas primarily serving students of color lack of access to high quality equitable education.

According the 2016 press release:

- Only a third of high schools with high Black and Latino enrollments offer calculus, compared to 56% of those that serve low numbers of Black and Latino students.
- Less than half the high schools with high Black and Latino enrollments offer physics, while two in three high schools that have low numbers of Black and Latino student offer physics.
- English learners have disproportionately low participation rates in Gifted and Talented Education (GATE) programs: while English learners are 11% of all students in schools offering GATE programs, fewer than 3% of GATE students nationwide are English learners.
- Black and Latino students also participate at lower rates in Gifted and Talented Education (GATE) programs. Although Black and Latino students make up 42% of students enrolled in schools that offer GATE programs, they are only 28% of the students who participate in those programs.

And access to experienced teaching staff is vastly different for students of color in urban schools compared to white peers.

- Ten percent of the teachers in schools with high numbers of Black and Latino students are in their first year of teaching, compared to only 5% in schools with low numbers of Black and Latino students.

- Eleven percent of black students, 9% of Latino students and 7% of American Indian or Alaska Native students attend schools where more than 20% of teachers are in their first year of teaching, compared to 5% of white students (U.S. Department of Education Office of Civil Rights, 2016).

Finally, returning to the First Look report highlights why I insist on *inclusive* anti-racist work particularly as it relates to students with disabilities. Consider the following:

> More than one out of five American Indian or Alaska Native (23%), Native Hawaiian or other Pacific Islander (23%), black (25%), and multiracial (27%) boys with disabilities served by the Individuals with Disabilities Education Act (IDEA) received one or more out-of-school suspensions, compared to one out of ten white (10%) boys with disabilities served by the IDEA. (U.S. Department of Education Office of Civil Rights, 2016, p. 9)

This summary data provides a glimpse of the inequities and injustices that are replicated again and again in our schools. (For recent data on your school and/or district see Appendix A: "How's My School District Doing.") Ill-formed and dangerous pedagogy and policy decisions are especially found in urban settings that primarily serve students of color. Thus, supporting inclusive anti-racist practice in urban schools seems particularly important.

The demographic dissonance between a teaching force that is overwhelmingly white and an increasingly racially diverse student body, is fairly common knowledge. Yet beyond noting this difference and coining phrases like the "achievement gap," little effort is made within schools to authentically engage at a personal, pedagogical, and curricular level the complex topics of race, racism, and racial identity. In attempting to disrupt some of these silences, this book seeks to provide resources for anti-racist teachers as they move beyond guilt, anger, shame, fear, marginalization, and isolation, into an empowered space of inspired learning and teaching for all.

This book rests on the premise that as a nation, the United States is far from post-racial. Critical race theorists put this best in arguing that racism is endemic in the United States and shapes all of our institutions. As an educator, I am particularly concerned with the ways that racism has shaped and continues to shape the policies, practices, and pedagogy found in our schools. We are bombarded by messages about how our schools are failing. But when we deconstruct those messages, it becomes clear that only some schools, some teachers, and some students are labeled as failing. The disproportionate emphasis on communities of color, the rhetoric of deficit that frames these communities as lacking and parents as not caring, the often-dysfunctional relationship between white educators and students of color, all help to illustrate the ways in which race continues to disrupt meaningful education for all students.

To address this, I aim to take into account the deeply human dimensions of anti-racist teaching, while drawing attention to the threat of burnout, inviting closer inspection of curricula development, and exploring tangible ways to sustain this important work for teaching. Additionally, through naming and exploring my own place of privilege as a white woman, I seek to engage readers in the importance of ongoing reflection and critical analysis of one's own biases and role one can play in either replicating or disrupting oppressive practices in schools.

A word about choices I make in this book. Ultimately, I wish to see schools become spaces where all students can thrive. I believe students must not be asked to check their multifaceted identities at the door. I strive to support teachers as they attempt to navigate the immediacy of students' interdependent identities, for no person is simply a race, class, gender, sexuality, or a disability. Our identities are complex and quality teaching must be ready to engage that complexity. Centering race in this work does not mean we ignore other aspects of students' identities or other forms of oppression. As bell hooks (2003) writes,

> Working to end racism in education is the only meaningful and lasting change that will benefit black students and all students. [...] Significantly anti-racist educational settings not only protect and nurture the self-esteem of all students, but also prepare students to live in a world that is diverse. (p. 80)

I choose to foreground anti-racist teaching because of the continued significance of race and the ongoing dominance and current resurgence of white supremacy in our country. This does not mean that other identities aren't significant. Terms like "anti-oppressive" reach to address all forms of dominance including racism; but don't center race. However, to ignore the variety of ways our identities are interdependent can also replicate forms of dominance. I call for *inclusive anti-racist pedagogy* and practice in an effort to center race without excluding other forms of identity.

Living in a racialized society results in all sorts of distortions, stereotypes, and misinformation about those seen as racially different from ourselves. When racial difference is coupled with other marginalized identities such as disability and/or LGBTQ identity, more distancing and labeling can result. These distortions can lead to multiple awkward moments in our classroom interactions. An inclusive anti-racist teacher must be willing to engage those moments, rather than glossing them over or rushing to more "normative" ground if we are to build liberatory communities. This is often not tidy work, but crucial nonetheless.

I had been teaching for several years in a large multi-racial, urban high school when one such moment presented itself. In my 10th grade English class we had been reading Sandra Cisneros' fabulous novel, *House on Mango Street* (1991). This collection of vignettes not only helped students understand a variety of literary devices, but the stories, told through the voice of Esperanza, an adolescent Latinx, provided a rich ground work for discussions of race, class, language, cultural identity, gender, and sexuality. The following interaction happened after reading one of the vignettes that dealt with Esperanza's dawning sexuality. In a moment that represents both the beauty and complexity of high school teaching, "Andrea" a white female student revealed that her mother was gay and that she herself is bisexual. Unbeknownst to me, "Andrea" was dating "Patrice," an African American female, in the class. The two had recently had an argument and were sitting apart from each other (something that was odd given they usually sat next to each other). As she talked, Andrea glared at Patrice and said, "Some people are ashamed to admit what they really are."

The glare and the pointed comments were not missed by anyone in the class. The class was silent for a moment and then a group of young men— white, Black, Hmong, and Latinx, began to laugh and someone called out, "Y'all some freaky people up in here." Sitting next to me was "Samantha" a soft-spoken African American student who frequently came to hang out in my room before class. She was crying. She whispered, "My Grandmother told me that was a sin..." She was close friends with both Andrea and Patrice. As the room settled back down, the bell rang and the students quickly filed out of the room. Patrice was slow to pack up her things and Samantha headed to my desk for tissues. The next class started in 5 minutes.

For those not familiar with the pace of a typical day in a school, this reality of crisis, regroup, and teach again might seem unbelievable. But for anyone who has worked in schools the reality is all too clear. When I was teaching high school I typically saw between 100–120 students throughout the day. Each group of 25–30 students would come to my class for 50 minutes a day, 5 days a week. I often joke with preservice teachers that teaching is the only profession that requires teachers to plan when they need to pee. As crass as that may sound, the truth is teachers are under tremendous pressure to keep things moving, to react to the unexpected, to engage all students, and (lest we forget) improve test scores. Given all of that, it might not be surprising that many teachers shy away from curricular choices and topics that may get messy. Certainly, had I chosen to teach *House on Mango Street* strictly as an example of literature that is highly effective in uses of powerful sensory imagery and a variety of other literary devices I might have avoided such an event altogether. (In Chapter 5, I discuss a missed opportunity with this text.) Yet, inclusive anti-racist work means engaging students where they are and providing opportunities for all in the class community to learn, grow, and change. Inclusive anti-racist pedagogy means teaching against oppression in all forms, but race is ever present in our world and is enmeshed with other issues.

As the earlier story demonstrates, I pull heavily on my own experiences and research throughout this text. For me, separating my own experience as if it is not a part of my own racial socialization is at best disingenuous and at worst replicates the very systems of oppression I rail against throughout the book. That said, as the white mother of a Black child (now adult) I paused about how much to share. Do I write regarding my experiences being a mother to my son? How will it be read? Do I need to shy away from using our family's encounters with the school system for risk of being dismissed as too personal, too tokenizing, too . . . ? In the end, I asked my son if I could share some stories about our family's experiences with racism in the schools. He told me, "People need to know." The stories I offer are one part of how I understand the world. My life as a white mother of a Black child does not give me a pass on racism or insulate me from white privilege. I offer the personal stories because they are a part of my life, not as some proof of my innate goodness or anti-racist credentials.

I also attempt to write from a place of humility. I say attempt, because writing about my own experiences, even the ones that are less than stellar examples, requires a fair bit of ego. Yet, I write with the full knowledge that without my teachers (professors, students, family, as well as writers and artists I will never meet) that opened up a larger world to me, this work is impossible. I write knowing that people of color have consistently named the racism and white supremacy I decry here, and have often been ignored, abused, and even murdered as a result of attempting to stand against such hate.

Words are created by symbols that together create meaning. I deliberately broke with stylistic rules and chose to write "white" and "whiteness" using a lower-case letter. I toyed with this both ways, but in the end, it is one very small, symbolic visual act in an attempt to decenter white always dominating with the proverbial capital W! Also, in terms of language, I sometimes slip into language that says "we" need to work towards change. As much as possible I have removed "we" voice unless it is very clear the "we" I am discussing. As a white woman, I am very aware that the use of "we" can obscure and deny voices on the margins. That said, no one can walk the inclusive anti-racist path alone.

The book combines theory and practice, examines history and the present moment, and is located inside and outside the classroom. The material included here includes personal, political, and theoretical understandings of inclusive anti-racist pedagogy and practice. Listed in the appendices of the book are activities, reflections, or reading lists that correspond to each chapter and can be used to reflect on both personal teachings as well as larger issues of pedagogy, policy, and practice.

Chapter 1, "Where *I'm* From—Where *We're* From—Where *They're* From: Stories of Race in the United States" sets the stage for the book by examining the personal, historical, and national stories told about race. Using my own story as a jumping off point I illustrate the differing ways race is the product of racism and how our nation's identity is tied up in a damaging racial mythology.

Chapter 2, "Fire in the Belly: Why Theory Matters" explores how theory is related to practice and examines two key theoretical lenses: Critical race theory and anti-racism that are core to this work. This chapter examines the problem with "color blindness" through the lens of theatre (and names the ableism within that term.) It also explains some key tenets of critical race theory and offers examples of anti-racist teaching in practice as well as a consideration of the difference between and ally and an accomplice towards racial justice.

Chapter 3, "Race, Disability, and Inclusion: We Have to Do This Together" expands the theoretical lens to include critical disability studies, and in doing so, forces an examination of the ways the term inclusion is used and abused. This chapter explores the history and current practices of exclusion based on race and disability and points out the intersection of ableism and racism. Too often, especially in the context of urban education, disability, and race are only discussed in terms of the problematic disproportionality of students of color (particularly Black students) being placed in special education programming. While that discussion is crucial, it is also important for urban educators to go further in their understandings and constructions of race and disability in order to challenge the racism and ableism present in many schools and classrooms. This chapter introduces the theoretical framework of "DisCrit" and debunks some of the myths around conceptions of inclusion.

Chapter 4, "When the Teacher Doesn't Know: White Knowledge, White Teachers, White Community, White Explanations," examines some of the consequences of racial miseducation. This chapter synthesizes some personal examples of racial miseducation and utilizes some of my own research into building inclusive anti-racist communities to explore the damage done to people of color when white explanations and white ignorance stands as the authority in the room. The chapter also explores the continued miseducation of white students regarding race and uses a case study to examine possibilities for disrupting this education. This chapter revisits concepts of inclusion and closes with some self-reflective questions a teacher might ask regarding their practice and their school.

Chapter 5, "Yes, That's Me!" in many ways is the "so what" of this book. It focuses on students and revisits the work of critical multicultural education.There is a sense in many academic circles that we have moved past the need to discuss and promote multiculturalism. While in Chapter 2 I critique divorcing practice from theory, here I urge teacher educators, teachers, and preservice teachers to recall that theory must also involve practice. While critical multiculturalism may not be new to many in the field, it is still emerging in many K–12 classrooms and often nonexistent in many college classrooms. Theory has outpaced practice and this chapter tries to bridge that gap. This chapter explores the impact of critical multiculturalism in practice and what happens when it is not in place. This chapter also revisits culturally relevant pedagogy, explores culturally responsive pedagogy, and stresses the continuing need for such an approach in all classrooms.

The final chapter, "Dangerous White Lady: The Need for Critical Community" revisits the opening of this book. It explores areas of growth and stagnation in my own inclusive anti-racist development, warns against particular pitfalls in this work, and urges readers to build *deliberate anti-racist communities.*

Resisting racism, agitating for change, and walking an inclusive anti-racist path requires commitment to unflinchingly look at one's failures and examine silences. It is work that must be done in all settings: rural, urban, and suburban. This book offers all preservice and in-service teachers some perspectives and reflections on engaging anti-racist inclusive practice. It may be particularly useful for in-service teachers working in urban schools or preservice teachers seeking to work in urban settings. The questions raised here ask each of us to consider our own positioning and interrogate the stories we tell ourselves about "the other." The book seeks to call in white teachers in particular to carefully examine our own biases and the ways we may replicate white supremacist ideology within our pedagogy and curricula. The questions posed here and the work ahead is not easy. This is work best taken on with those that can challenge with love and help support one other as we imagine and work towards a more just world. I engage this fight for inclusive racial justice because I see no other path. So, let's begin again.

Acknowledgments

This book is possible because of the support of many. First and foremost, thanks to my husband, Stephen Hoffman, who while working on his own healing, cared for me through a lengthy and debilitating illness. He propped me up and kept me writing bit by bit and continues to be my cheerleader and central source of support.

Thanks to Renee Affolter and Jason Gingold (and my amazing nieces Josie, Lily, and Phoebe) who continually shared their home with us over the years—caring for us, giving up bedrooms and helping us through multiple housing transitions.

Thanks to my teachers, past and present for inspiring me to think, act, question, teach, and challenge. In particular, thanks to Gloria Ladson-Billings and Stacey Lee for your work and for believing in this teacher. Thanks to my former students (who are also my teachers) from Champaign, Madison, and Middlebury. Special thanks to Maya Doig-Acuña and Ali Muldrow for sharing their poetry.

Thank you to Deborah Hoffman who models inclusive anti-racist practice, generosity, sisterhood, and friendship and inspires us all.

A world of gratitude to Thandeka K. Chapman for taking a risk, for always being the best part of AERA, and for feedback rooted in love. And to Jamel K. Donnor and Lisa Louztenheiser for not giving up on that one graduate school friend who took longer to get it together.

Through the Fog, pages xxvii–xxviii
Copyright © 2019 by Information Age Publishing
xxvii

Thank you to Julie Causton, Susanne and Pete Benton, George Theo-haris, Susan Burch, Claudia Cooper, Jonathan Miller-Lane, Tracy Weston, Christal Brown, Gabby Arca, the Ward family, and Middlebury Posse 13, for all of the laughs, support, friendship, and gentle prodding along the way. Thanks to Scout and Hermione for all the tail wags and head clearing walks in the woods.

To my parents, Nancy and Gary Affolter, thank you for making it ok to question and for never wavering in your love of our family. To my siblings Renee Affolter, Dana Fowler, Gary Affolter, I think much of my desire to see a better world is rooted in the laughter of our childhood, the scheming in the tree house, and the pageantry of our backyard plays—all kids should get a chance to be kids.

Finally, to my son, Jerry Hoffman: I will always be your mama bear.

1

Where I'm *From—Where* We're *From—Where* They're *From*

Stories of Race in the United States

It ain't nothing to find no starting place in the world. You just start from where you find yourself.

—August Wilson, *Joe Turner's Come and Gone*, 1988

Home Truths

For most of my adult life I have loathed the moment in social conversation when asked, "So, where are you from?" I usually opt for the regional reference, "the Midwest," in the hope we can move on to safer or more interesting terrain. However, this is often not enough so I say, "I have lived in a lot of different places, but my childhood was spent in Central Illinois." Usually this is both vague and specific enough. It is on those rare cases where people know the area well enough that I start to panic. They start guessing town names: Peoria? Morton? Tremont? If they are that close, I just tell them, "Pekin, Illinois."

Through the Fog, pages 1–14
Copyright © 2019 by Information Age Publishing

1

For most readers this means nothing, but there are enough people who know that part of Pekin's fame has nothing to do with the welcome sign claiming Pekin as the "Marigold Capital of the World." Rather, Pekin is known for once having one of the nation's most racist high school team names: "The Chinks." Local historians explain that this name was meant to make a specific reference to its namesake, "Peking" (a mispronunciation of Beijing, China). Reasons for the link are unclear to begin with, but it isn't uncommon to hear the myth that if one started in Pekin and traced longitudinally around the Earth, s/he would end up in present day Beijing.

Up until 1975, the team mascots, a white boy ("the Chink") and white girl ("the Chinkette"), dressed in someone's idea of traditional Chinese peasant attire, would enter the basketball court or football field and bow towards the opposing team before each sporting event started. This practice, along with the use of the team name, was discontinued while I was in early elementary school. I know most of this history through talking with my parents who attended Pekin schools during the heyday of the team name.

My only direct memory related to this name has to do with my mother. One unusually warm spring day when I was still young enough to enjoy splashing around in the wading pool stationed on our side patio, a group of "big kids" approached my mom from the sidewalk. They had a clipboard in hand and asked her to sign a petition. She stood and talked with them and said "no" and walked back to my sisters and me. When I asked her what that was all about, she said, "They wanted me to sign a petition that said the school should keep the team name. I told them no." I must have asked why. "That name hurts people's feelings. It is mean. I wish someone had told me it was so mean. But now I know and we can't call a team that or use that word."

I was recently telling my father about using the story of our hometown in this book. He told me another story that perfectly illustrates why anti-racist education is crucial for all students. He was in his first year of college when he received news that his high school team had won a basketball state championship. Thrilled and proud of his alma mater he approached a group of young men at a party and announced, "How about those Chinks! They did it!" One of the guys in the group immediately told my father, "You racist son of a bitch. Why would you say that?" More words were exchanged and just at the point of a fight, the other man explained to my father the racism behind the word. It stopped my Dad in his tracks. He told me, "I was shocked. I had no idea. I felt so stupid and I never used that word again." As we talked, though, it was clear to me why the moment made such a lasting impression on him. He felt betrayed by his town, his teachers, and the adults he had trusted. He asked me, "Why would they knowingly teach us that?"

Why would they knowingly teach us that? It was mean. I didn't know. I am struck by the honesty of my mother and the shock and hurt of my father. What I learned in both situations is important for my work as an anti-racist teacher. If we are white, we won't often notice the racism and hurt we are inflicting and often won't do the right thing to resist racism. But we can always learn and once we know more, we must change.

What does it mean to come from a town that once had a virulently racist name for a team mascot and had a reputation as a sundown town? Since about 1890 and continuing until 1968, white Americans barred African Americans from thousands of towns across the United States, especially in the North. "These are called sundown towns because of posted signs in many of them warning African Americans to not 'let the sun go down on you in [name of town]'" (Loewen, 2010, p. 192).

Sundown towns were enforced by both explicit signs like the one described above, but also through reputation, as was and continues to be the case with Pekin. Throughout his work, but especially in the text, *Sundown Towns: A Hidden Dimension of American Racism*, Loewen (2006), excavates the racism and the history of sundown in Northern cities that often escapes examination of blatant racism. Understanding personal stories and histories of race and finding the history underlying hometowns, especially for white anti-racists is important. (A link that explores sundown towns and some guiding questions related to those findings are provided in Appendix B.)

Growing up in that town shaped my resistance to racism in particular ways. I learned from my parents that "we don't treat people that way" and that people that used words like the n-word were bad and ignorant. I learned that if words hurt other people, we weren't to use them. I learned to watch out for racists, but I learned little about what racism meant beyond overt acts. My classmates were white, our family friends were white, and my family was white. My learning was, and is incomplete, but going further is not impossible.

I dreaded sophomore English. For some reason all sophomores were required, over the course of the year, to complete a series of speeches: a demonstration speech, a persuasive speech, and some passage of memorized Shakespeare.

My new English teacher, Mrs. Smith's (not her real name) attention in class inevitably went to the coolest of the cool kids—members of the boys' basketball team. For some reason my class was full of them and they seemed to have any number of inside jokes and shared experiences to fill most of each class with witty banter. The rest of us were left to our own devices as long as our antics did not detract from planning the next cookout at Mrs. Smith's place or the recounting of the latest basketball game. But when it came to the persuasive speeches, I must have missed the memo.

The week of the persuasive speeches dawned. I recall listening to the speeches and determining that they had little to do with me. Until *the* speech happened. I suppose I should have seen it coming. Sure enough, one of the white male athletes (let's call him Bob) decided to give his speech on why changing the name of our sports team (years ago when we were children) from Chinks to Dragons was silly and that it undermined tradition.

I remember being shocked. I kept looking around to try to see Mrs. Smith's expression or trying to catch the eyes of my classmates. When Bob finished there was the usual perfunctory clapping that followed each speech and then Mrs. Smith's voice, "Bob, I really commend you for taking on a controversial topic. Really well done." That night I scrubbed the speech I was going to give on the inequity of funding for women's sports and instead wrote a speech on "prejudice." I named the history of racism in our town and I called out the history of the team name for what it was: narrow-minded, racist, and yes, mean. When I finished, my face beet red and hands still shaking, the class was silent. Mrs. Smith looked up from her desk and shook her head in disgust. She made eye contact with Bob and then uttered, "Well, that was depressing." I learned that day that white people aren't really supposed to talk about race and they really aren't supposed to notice or name racism. I also learned that day that I didn't really care about those rules anymore.

Considering the stories that shape understandings of race, power, and privilege are crucial in the development of inclusive anti-racist teaching. We are born into a world that gives us distorted information about our fellow human beings. In the United States this often means that, if we are white, we are fed racist messages that warp our views of communities of color and lead us further away from racial equity and justice. We have no control over where we are born and little control over the communities in which we are raised. However, we can work to educate ourselves, challenge our assumptions, and reach outside of our known communities. We must do this in order to build inclusive communities in which we don't fear or ignore our differences but rather utilize them as keys to deepening and expanding our understandings about the world and ourselves. (For personal exploration of miseducation, please see Appendix B: "Reflective Activities on the Stories of Race.")

The Story of Race and the Creation of the White World

Like our economic and political worlds, stories too are defined by the principle of nkali. How they are told, who tells them, when they are told, how many stories are told, are really dependent upon power. Power is the ability not just to tell the story of another person, but also to make it the definitive story of that person.

—Chimamanda Adichie, *The Danger of a Single Story,* 2009

Social scientists have long argued that race, as commonly understood in the United States, is not a biological reality, but a social construct. The racial titles we give to one's skin tone, hair texture, eye color, and other phenotypical markers are imbued with social meanings, not biological realities. In 2000, scientists Francis Collins and Craig Venter attended a White House reception where they reported their findings on sequencing the human genome (the complete sequence of DNA): 99.9% of all human genome sequences are identical. The concept of race deployed in the United States withstands no serious scientific rigor. There are no distinct "races" of humankind. Since the early 1970s scientists have shown that:

> . . .the vast proportion of genetic diversity (85 to 90 percent) occurs *within* so-called races (i.e., within Asians or Africans) and only a minor proportion (7 percent) between racial groups . . . (Mukherjee, 2016, p. 342)

Instead of conceiving of race as a biological fact, scholars Omi and Winant (2015) urge us to see race as a category that is unstable and "constantly being transformed by political struggle." Yet the concept of race remains deeply rooted in a biological mythology that has been operationalized for white political and power gain. Indeed, throughout U.S. history being able to determine who could be considered white has been crucial for preserving white privilege and white dominance. In this way we can begin to understand that racism begat racial categories. *RACE DOES NOT EXIST OUTSIDE OF RACISM.*

Thomas Jefferson, who was revered for penning the famous words, "All men are created equal . . ." can also be credited for having a significant hand in creating and defining racial categories and hierarchies that shaped U.S. racism. For example, in "Notes From the State of Virginia" (1785) Jefferson writes,

> The blacks, whether originally a distinct race, or made distinct by time and circumstances, are inferior to the whites in the endowments both of body and mind. It is not against experience to suppose, that different species of the same genus, or varieties of the same species, may possess different quali-

fications. Will not a lover of natural history then, one who views the grada-
tions in all the races of animals with the eye of philosophy, excuse an effort
to keep those in the department of man as distinct as nature has formed
them? (http://historytools.davidjvoelker.com/sources/Jefferson-Race.pdf)

Jefferson was not alone in his scientific racism. In 1779, German physician
Johann Fredrick Blumenbach, used his study of human skulls (craniology)
to divide humans into five races: Caucasian, Mongolian, Ethiopian, American, and Malay.

It is worth noting that while most of the terms have fallen out of favor, the term Caucasian can still be heard and is used as a racial category
regularly. I strongly urge abolishing Caucasian as a term to describe race. It
merely continues to elevate a category rooted in scientific racism and white
supremacy. A look at the history of the term Caucasian is illustrative of the
depths and sickness of white supremacy.

One of the most bizarre aspects of the creation of these racial categories is Blumenbach's reasoning for using the term "Caucasian." Blumenbach considered the skull in his collection that belonged to a Georgian
woman to be the most beautiful. He writes,

> I have taken the name of this variety from Mount Caucasus because both the
> neighborhood, and especially the southern slope produces the most beauti-
> ful race of men, . . . the most beautiful form of the skull from which as from a
> mean and primeval type, others diverge. . . . Besides it is white in color, which
> we may fairly assume to be the primitive color of mankind . . . it is very easy
> to degenerate into brown, but very much more difficult for dark to become
> white. (as cited in quoted in Jacobson, 2001, p. 1)

It is difficult to follow this logic. Somehow, the prettiest skull was the one
that remained the whitest and thus represented the origin of man as well
as the highest "race" of man. Blumenbach's work influenced the work of
white U.S. scientists and helped construct new forms of white supremacy.
Closely adhering to Blumenbach's racial categories, U.S. physician Samuel
Morton (who also studied skulls to determine "race") attached physical, intellectual, and emotional traits to each racial category. He published these
findings in *Crania Americana* in 1839.

Passages of Morton's work quoted here were found in the Facing History and Ourselves publication, *Race and Membership in American History:
The Eugenics Movement*. Facing History produces publications with students
and teachers in mind and is a fabulous resource for those seeking some
accessible readings and hands-on exercises for students. More complete
citation information can be found in the bibliography.

He describes Caucasians as having "naturally fair skin" with "well-proportioned features" (Facing History and Ourselves, 2002, p. 47). He continues that "this race is distinguished for the facility with which it attains the highest intellectual endowments" (Facing History and Ourselves, 2002, p. 47). From here Morton moves to describe the "lesser races." In each, note the ways he frames the deficits of each group in implicit comparison to the "superior" Caucasian.

Asians (whom he refers to as Mongolians) were characterized as having "sallow or olive colored skin which appears to be drawn tight over the bones of the face" (Facing History and Ourselves, 2002, p. 48). He continues, "in their intellectual character the Mongolians are ingenious, imitative, and highly susceptible of cultivation." He notes, "So versatile are their feelings and actions, that they have been compared to the monkey race, whose attention is perpetually changing from one object to another. . . ." (Facing History and Ourselves, 2002, p. 48). Casting Asians as less human and at times a threat to white jobs and safety gave way to numerous laws and actions against Asians throughout our country's history. A propaganda poster from the 1800s warns against the threat of Chinese men to white racial purity with a white woman used to signify this purity. In the image a man dressed in an exaggerated traditional Chinese costume and hairstyle stands astride a white woman who is either dead or unconscious on the ground. The man's left hand holds a large smoking pistol, his right hand holds a lit torch, and he grips a large knife in his teeth. The words "The Yellow Terror in all His Glory" are typed beneath the picture (Sociology Images, 2014). The message is clear these people are foreign, scary, and dangerous and must be stopped by whites in order to preserve and protect white purity.

Such anti-Asian sentiment laid the groundwork for events like the 1871 Chinese Massacre in which 500 non-Asian men and women swarmed the "Chinatown" area of Los Angeles and hunted down and lynched 15 Chinese immigrants (one of the largest mass lynchings in U.S. history) and killed another four by other means—no one was held accountable for these crimes. Or the Chinese Exclusion Act of 1892 which halted all Chinese immigration and denied citizenship to Chinese people, and Executive Order 9066 which, in 1942, after Pearl Harbor, authorized the deportation and incarceration of 120,000 of Japanese descent (many of whom were U.S. citizens). Racism became part of school policies directed against non-whites (particularly Chinese), such as California School Law of 1860 which "segregated children of Black, Chinese, and Indian descent into separate schools" (Kuo, 1998, p. 190). Local press celebrated such acts as a way to protect the white race:

> [The codes] let us keep our public schools free from the intrusion of the inferior races. If we are compelled to have Negroes and Chinamen among us, it is better, of course, that they should be educated. But teach them separately from our own children. Let us preserve our Caucasian blood pure. We want no mongrel race of moral and mental hybrids to people the mountains and valleys of California. (as quoted in Kuo, 1998, p. 190)

Note the use of "mongrel race" in the above passage. Clearly, scientific racism and the specter of tainting the white "race" with "other" (non-white blood) was present. Far from being an isolated thought exercise, Morton's racial categorizations had a profound impact on the formation and perpetuation of white racial dominance.

Morton (Facing History and Ourselves, 2002) writes, "the American Race is marked by a brown complexion; long, black, lank hair, and a deficient beard" (p. 48). He continues listing perceived deficits of this group stating, "In their mental character the Americans are averse to cultivation, and slow in acquiring knowledge; restless, revengeful and fond of war…" (p. 48). Morton's overall assessment of the "Americans" include "their mental faculties, from infancy to old age present a continued childhood… [they] are not only averse to restraints of education, but for the most part are incapable of a continued process of reasoning on abstract subjects" (p. 48). Here again we see the categorization of those deemed as non-white as less human and less deserving of the same protections and respect granted to whites. The atrocities carried out by whites against Native Americans dates to the arrival of the first white man in what is now the United States. Native Americans were seen as such a threat to the "rights" of whites to colonize the land that attempts to overtly eliminate them included Sir Jeffrey Amherst, Commander in Chief of the British Forces in North America advising his subordinates, "You will do well to try to inoculate the Indians [with smallpox] by means of blankets, as well as to try every other method, that can serve to extirpate this execrable race" (United to End Genocide, n.d., para. 10).

Early colonists were given monetary rewards for each scalp of a Native person they produced. Pricing was scaled: 50 pounds for an adult male scalp to 20 for the scalps of children under the age of 12 (Newsom & Bissonette-Lewis, 2012). When murder was seen as too harsh, attempts were made to "civilize them." Carlisle Indian Industrial School founder, Captain Richard H. Pratt stated the goal was that, "all the Indian there is in the race should be dead. Kill the Indian in him, and save the man" (1892/1973). Such efforts included removing children from their homes and parents, cutting their hair, changing their names to Anglo names, punishing children for speaking their home language, and teaching children that the ways of their families were savage and wrong. Native parents were seen as unfit and it wasn't until 1978, with the passage of the Indian Child Welfare Act that parents were given some protections about the removal of their children from their homes and community. The message that whites know best, and modeling one's life and customs after Anglo traditions is loud and clear in the treatment of Native Americans and their children.

Morton (Facing History and Ourselves, 2002) reserves some of his most racist observations for what he terms the African or Negro race. He begins that this race is "characterized by a black complexion, and black woolly hair, the eyes are large and prominent, the nose broad and flat, the lips thick, and the mouth wide" (pp. 48–49). Tellingly, given the prevalence of slavery, Morton stresses, "Negroes are proverbially fond of their amusements, in which they engage with great exuberance of spirit; and a day of toil is with them no bar to a night of revelry" (p. 49). He also emphasizes, "Negroes are the lowest forms of humanity" (p. 49). Our country's Founding Fathers certainly appear to have embraced this assertion in laws such as the Three-Fifths Compromise of 1787, in which enslaved Black people were counted as three-fifths of a person when determining political representation for states. The irony here is that white slave owners wanted enslaved people to be counted the same as whites so that the Southern states could have an upper hand in government. In all instances, enslaved Blacks were treated as property, but on paper, when it came to the Constitutional Congress and representational power, slave owners wanted "their property" to be counted as people. Mind you, these people were not afforded freedom and would not benefit in any way from this compromise. Our country is built on a white supremacist system that morphs in every way possible to continue to deny the humanity of Blacks and other people of color. The country is built on the mythology of racial categories—a mythology that has promoted white racial purity and superiority at the cost of all else. From slavery, to Jim Crow laws, to disenfranchisement of Black voters, to murder of unarmed Black men and women and children by police and private citizens—the United States has repeatedly found ways to replicate white supremacy in policy and in practice.

Upon reading *Crania Americana* (Facing History and Ourselves, 2002), abolitionist, scholar, and former slave, Frederick Douglass, attempted to point out how the findings were shaped by "prejudice rather than from facts." He continues,

> It is the province of prejudice to blind; and scientific writers, no less than others, write to please, as well as to instruct, and even unconsciously themselves, (sometimes) sacrifice what is true to what is popular. Fashion is not

confined to dress; but extends to philosophy as well—and it is fashionable now, in our land, to exaggerate the differences between the Negro and the European. (Foner, as cited in Facing History and Ourselves, 2002, p. 52)

Not surprisingly, whites largely ignored Douglass' critique. Morton's work significantly supported white supremacy and influenced white journalists, politicians, and ministers. This pseudo-science provided justification for the genocide and displacement of Native Americans and the enslavement of African Americans. If African Americans were, according to Morton, "the lowest forms of humanity," and Native Americans are perpetual children incapable of rational thought, it was easier to overlook the protections of the Constitution because clearly "all men being created equal" did not apply to those "lesser people." There was no moral quandary for whites because clearly "science" backed up the systemic degradation of people of color. And this of course is not an historical artifact.

One can trace the stories told by whites that justified subjugation, exploitation, and murder of people of color, but those stories are not just a distant memory. With such a history, one can begin to see how modern issues—poisoned drinking water of a primary Black population in Flint, Michigan; police violence against Native water defenders in North Dakota; anti-immigrant laws against Latinos (among other groups); travel bans on people from Muslim countries; attacks on Muslim-Americans; mass-incarceration of Black and Brown men and women; police violence and murder of Black men, women, and children—become possible. If the master script of the country is that white is right—it doesn't matter that this rightness is rooted in debunked science, what matters is the protection of white racial superiority, protection that numerous "other" groups are denied.

The demarcation and creation of racial categories in order to promote racism and continue to privilege white, wealthy, non-disabled, U.S. *citizens* is perhaps clearest when one considers the Eugenics movement. This pseudoscientific movement popular in the late 19th and early 20th century was based on the belief "of inherent genetic worth" of some groups over others and sought to "improve the human species" via selective reproduction and sterilization. (Burch, 2009, p. 333).

Eugenics and the Threat of the White Woman

To chronicle all of the horrors the eugenics movement inflicted on marginalized groups (poor, disabled, people of color) is beyond the scope of this book. For this chapter, what is crucial to understand is that white America built a story that justified subjugation and employed racist science to construct who could be considered pure, healthy, and white—and thus worthy of protection.

Eugenics supported and expanded existing laws against interracial marriage and emphasized concerns about mixing of "races" (miscegenation). Influential eugenicists like Madison Grant warned that mixing of races was a "social and racial crime." In his widely read text, *The Passing of the Great Race* (1916), Grant asserted,

> The cross between a white man and an Indian is an Indian; the cross between a white man and a negro is a negro.... When it becomes thoroughly understood that the children of mixed marriages between contrasted races belong to the lower type, the importance of transmitting in unimpaired purity the blood inheritance of ages will be appreciated at its full value. (as quoted in Lombardo, n.d., para. 3)

Such thinking led to strict anti-miscegenation laws. Virginia's Racial Integrity Act of 1924 is one chilling example. This Act made interracial marriage illegal and included strict parameters as to who could qualify as white. The law illustrates the absurdity of racist science by insisting that "the term 'white person' shall apply only to such person as to have no trace whatever of any blood other than Caucasian" (Lombardo, n.d., para. 7).

Virginia was following a national trend in which whiteness was perceived to be under threat and in need of protection. This trend that has never really ceased, just morphed over time—witness the successful campaign of Trump who promised to "make America Great again," and appealed to the base fears of whites that *their* country was being taken away.

Numerous methods from eugenic sterilization, to racialized terror, to current policies that privilege whites, have been used overly and covertly in the defense of and protection of the "white race." One consistent rationalization for continued racism is the need to preserve the "sanctity" of white women. White women have been continually held up as the pure racial ideal in need of protection.

In the 1890s, Daniel G. Brinton, president of the American Association for the Advancement of Science, declared it a sacred mission to secure the purity of white women. He asserted, "Philanthropy is false ... religion is rotten, which would sanction a white woman enduring the embrace of a colored man," (as quoted in Lombardo, 2016, p. 297).

The atrocities committed in the name of white women are as baffling as they are horrifying. The white supremacist who murdered nine people "during a mass shooting at a prayer meeting at the Emmanuel African Methodist Episcopal Church in Charleston, South Carolina, shouted, 'Y'all are raping our white women, y'all are taking over the world'" (Sack & Binder, 2016, p. A1).

Roof was hardly unique in using the excuse of protecting white women as a reason to go on such a hateful crusade. Protecting the purity of white women has been used again and again to justify murder, lynching, and other forms of violence and exclusion. One need only to look at a photograph of the mutilated face of Emmett Till, the 14-year-old boy from Chicago, who was tortured and murdered in 1955 in Mississippi for allegedly flirting with a white woman, for more proof of such horror. And the fact of white women participating and supporting such actions has often been overlooked. (As an example of this, do a search for Emmitt Till—his murderers' names are easily found. But it takes some digging to find the woman's name, whose purity was supposedly threatened when Emmitt Till said, "Bye-bye" to her after buying candy. *She* reported that a child had besmirched her honor. *She* put Emmitt Till's murder in motion with full knowledge of how her honor and purity would be protected.) White women have been used to prop up white supremacy, but they have also participated and continue to participate in such a regime.

White Teachers

To illustrate the modern-day version of offering white women perpetuating white supremacy, I offer some examples that relate to education. The first is a more general observation regarding the teacher demographics.

Women make up 76% of the total teaching force and 82% of the teaching force is white (Goldring, Taie, & Riddles, 2014). Meanwhile, students of color are the majority in many public schools. This alone would not necessarily be a concern if the parade of disproportionality did not accompany it. In our nation's schools, students of color experience inequity and discrimination in nearly every arena: *discipline*—higher suspension and expulsion rates than their white peers (Hoffman, 2014); *class placement*—less access to advanced level courses that require high order thinking (Oakes, 1985) and more likely to be labeled and placed in the most restrictive special education classes (Blanchett, 2006); *curricula*—Eurocentric curricula that celebrate whiteness while erasing and diminishing the accomplishments of people of color (see for example, Paris & Alim, 2014); and *academic achievement*—Black and Latino students have drop-out rates nearly double that of their white peers (Stetser & Stillwell, 2014) and more likely to have unqualified and/or ineffective teachers (Donnor, 2013).

To place all this at the feet of white women teachers alone is unfair and inaccurate. There are, of course, larger political systems in place that de-skill and disempower all teachers. From required high stakes testing to scripted curricula, teachers are increasingly treated not as educated professionals, but rather as robots commanded to do whatever it takes to produce high test scores from their students. Additionally, as a nation, we have turned our backs on key social issues that impact our students in many of our schools. Lack of quality health care, stable housing, access to healthy food and living wages are just some of the problems that disproportionately impact poor communities of color. (I hesitate to even use the term disproportionate as it suggests there is an amount that is an acceptable portion of neglect and racism. But it is a term that captures the discrepancies that are a result of white supremacist policies and practices.) It is ludicrous to think that these struggles don't impact students in the classroom and even more ridiculous to blame communities of color for such inequity. Such systemic racism is a result of larger policy implications supporting whiteness and rooted in neglect and disregard for fellow human beings. These issues are the result of more than the disproportionate number of white women in our public and charter school classrooms.

Even with that significant caveat, one must wonder about some of the practices in place in schools that police student behavior and militarize schools. From metal detectors to armed police officers, schools with diverse racial demographics increasingly look and feel like prisons. Black children represent only 18% of students enrolled in preschool yet make up 48% of students suspended from school more than once (U.S. Department of Education Office for Civil Rights, 2014). At 3 and 4 years old we are already telling children they don't fit and that schools aren't a place for them. Nationally, at all grade levels Black students are suspended at a rate 3 times higher than white students. Black students "represent 27% of students referred to law enforcement and 31% of students subjected to a school-related arrest" (U.S. Department of Education Office for Civil Rights, 2014, para. 6).

Much school discipline initiates with teacher office referrals. Skiba, Michael, Nardo, and Peterson (2002) examined the differences between white and Black students' office referrals and found that

> the majority of reasons for which white students are referred more frequently seem to be based on an objective event (e.g., smoking, vandalism) that leaves a permanent product. Reasons for black referrals to the office, on the other hand, are infractions (e.g., loitering, excessive noise) that would seem to require a good deal more subjective judgment on the part of the referring agent. Even the most serious of the reasons for office referrals among black students, *threat*, is dependent on perception of threat by the staff making the referral. (p. 334)

All of this raises questions regarding who matters in schools. Who is being protected and who is being criminalized? Who is cast as insubordinate or as a threat and who is understood in the classroom? Who is allowed to be a child in school and who is deemed criminal and dangerous for exhibiting the same behaviors? What happens when there is a disconnect between teacher and student? What happens when a student's actions are misread and misunderstood? Who pays the price?

2

Theoretical Underpinnings

Fire in the Belly

Teachers need to be intensely aware of what they value, what they honor, what they stand for. Even with this awareness, the machinery of schooling works on teachers like water on a rock: it wears us down, shapes us, and smooths us. Soon, if we're not careful, our lives make a mockery of our values. Resisting this fate involves conscious struggle, an attempt to find allies among the students, the parents, the teachers, and the citizenry. It requires collective action. It requires wedding consciousness to conduct and it involves taking responsibility for ourselves, for our work, for the world we see and can understand, and a world that could be but is not yet.

—William Ayers, 2004

I currently teach undergraduate students and occasionally work with in-service teachers. It is not uncommon to hear complaints from both groups regarding the study of theory. The complaints usually fall along the lines of "this is fine in *theory*, but in real life. . . ." The sentence is completed with a story about a student, classroom, or community where the theoretical just doesn't seem "useful" in the face of the day to day reality of a classroom. The problem with such a bifurcation is that theory undergirds practices.

Through the Fog, pages 15–44

What we believe about the world and especially about our students and communities impacts our practice in significant ways.

For example, the dominant theoretical framework of education in the United States is largely steeped in a model of meritocracy. This is the idea that all can succeed by working hard and those that work the hardest are objectively the best and the brightest. These individuals will rightfully reap the biggest rewards. This supports the capitalist model of competition so much so that getting ahead of others, rather than looking out for one another, is what is taught, modeled, and desired. In such a model a certain amount of failure and unequal outcomes is not only expected, but welcomed. After all, not all can succeed because then how can one determine the most deserving, the best, and the brightest? Acting from a theoretical underpinning of meritocracy leads one to cling to a notion of "radical individualism" that ignores the reality that one never succeeds or fails alone (Parker, 2003). Belief in meritocracy attributes all success: from professional prestige, academic credentials, financial well-being, and so forth, to the unique gifts and hard work of the individual while ignoring that such success is deeply intertwined with communities and institutions. A radical individualist fed on a belief of meritocracy only looks out for her own "people." In the classroom this means that any problem or perceived lack of achievement is located within students. Pedagogy, institutional barriers, cultural differences have nothing to do with said failure. A reliance and sole focus on the individual (driven by a belief in meritocracy) can lead a teacher to subscribe to deficit model explanations and thus decide the student and her family are not hard working, don't care about education, are not a "good fit" for a particular course of study, or are disengaged because of lack of ability or intellect. This vision of schooling drives many policy decisions and impacts the way "reform" of schools is framed around test scores.

The irony of course is in this supposedly neutral education system some students are subject to a regime of high stakes tests, scripted curricula, and rote learning inside classrooms that are ill-equipped and in buildings that often resemble prisons. While other students are offered classes with engaging and challenging material; encouraged to think critically; have access to high quality college preparation and arts programs; are provided adequate materials, new books, field trips, and so on; and learn in inviting physical spaces. A belief in meritocracy provides the theoretical underpinning to never name the inequities "some students" face, nor recognize the privileges offered to "other students." A belief in this myth of meritocracy allows one to continue to promote the notion that individuals succeed based on merit, skill, and hard work, without ever examining the conditions in which this supposed success takes place, or the interdependent nature of success.

The myth becomes that a student rises or falls alone when nothing could be further than the truth. Theory matters and it is intimately connected with what one does in the classroom.

In his foundational text on critical pedagogy, *The Pedagogy of the Oppressed*, Paulo Freire (1970/2018) writes against the separation of theory from practice. Here he examines the essence of interaction between humans: *the word*. He writes, "within the word we find two dimensions, reflection and action" (p. 75). He calls the interaction between reflection and action, praxis. One without the other does not work. A word without action (as in theory in isolation) is "idle chatter" (p. 75). Likewise, when action is taken without reflection, it becomes action for action's sake, an exercise devoid of larger meaning or work towards positive change. Specifically, "to exist is to name the world, to change it" (p. 76). Further this action and reflection must be done in dialogue with others. It is not the role of some in positions of power to name and diagnose a problem and others to be on the receiving end of this belief. Freire writes,

> Dialogue cannot occur between those who want to name the world and those who do not wish this naming—between those who deny other men the right to speak their word and those whose right to speak has been denied. (p. 76)

Splitting oneself from reflection, denying theory, especially as one goes about the work of building an inclusive classroom can only lead to replicating various forms of enforced silence and dominance. For me keeping anti-racism and critical race theory at the forefront of my core beliefs helps me as I work for "a world that could be but is not yet." I explain both of these concepts here as I situate my racial understanding.

Building the Fire: Anti-Racism

Anti-racism must be distinguished from non-racism. Many white people disassociate and try to distance themselves from overt racism (though this has shifted more since the 2016 election of Donald Trump). Instead of anti-racism, non-racism encompasses the thinking and actions of many whites. In a non-racist approach overt racism is rejected, racism is largely defined as obvious individual acts of meanness, forms of institutional racism are placed as artifacts of history rather than active policy, color blindness is celebrated, and systemic racism is ignored. Further acts of racism are frequently defined as *not* racist because of professed racial innocence on the part of whites (King & Chandler, 2016). A non-racist might decry extreme and overt racism, but will do nothing further.

Beverly Tatum (2008) offers an analogy that might shed light on the discomfort some people feel with the term anti-racist. She invites the reader to imagine racism as a moving sidewalk, like one in an airport. Active racists are walking fast on this sidewalk. Non-racists, the ones that are *nice*, don't use those words, and don't laugh at racist jokes are standing still and not actively participating in overt racism. Yet they are still being moved along to the same racist outcomes. Only those that actively resist by turning in the other direction and walking briskly in that opposite direction are embodying antiracism. Unless one actively resists, one is carried along and participates in the racism. Saying one isn't racist by doing nothing—by neither adding to overt racism or actively finding ways to disrupt systemic racism—is an exercise in moral self-congratulation and effectively contributes to the perpetuation of white supremacy.

This use of a moving sidewalk may give a glimpse at why some bristle at the suggestion that avoiding actively being racist is enough. After all, not being hostile or dismissive to those that one deems "different," avoiding racist language and racist jokes, or refusing to endorse friends' or relatives' racist thinking are all outward actions against racism. And while those stances are important, white anti-racists must understand there is more to do. Only actively moving in the opposite direction, working against racism (and not just shaking your head as you watch *those* white racists do things), examining your privileges and positions, challenging institutional, pedagogical, and curricular issues that contribute the perpetuation of racism in this country, and being willing to stand with marginalized communities without demanding to lead: only then is one engaging in anti-racist practice. I will examine specific examples of anti-racist education later in this chapter but first I need to define the theory that moved me from being non-racist to actively anti-racist: critical race theory.

Feeding the Fire: Critical Race Theory

> Our system of race is like a two-headed hydra. One head consists of outright racism—the oppression of some people on grounds of who they are. The other head consists of white privilege—a system by which whites help and buoy each other up. If one lops off a single head, say, outright racism, but leaves the other intact, our system of white over black/brown will remain virtually unchanged. (Delgado & Stefancic, 2012, p. 88)

My anti-racist development is greatly informed by critical race theory (CRT). I was first exposed to this theory in graduate school and studying it positively shifted my worldview and work towards anti-racist practice. The theory (and the theory in practice) take an unrelenting look at how racism shapes this country. But the theory doesn't stop with naming the reality of the endemic nature of racism, instead it uses that truth and builds from there.

CRT emerged in the 1970s when legal scholars such as Derrick Bell and Alan Freeman became frustrated with the glacial pace of racial justice re-form in the United States. These scholars noted that the standard practice of filing briefs, protesting, and appealing to people's moral code or good will produced fewer and fewer positive results.

CRT grew out of critical legal studies (CLS). CLS shares with CRT a cri-tique of the way the law in practice functions to benefit only the privileged and powerful while ignoring the needs of the poor. For CRT scholars, this critique of the law did not go far enough and ignored the racialized nature of the law and the disparate punitive impact the law had (and continues to have) on communities of color. (For foundational examples explaining this need for a critical racial analysis see, for example: Bell, 1992; Crenshaw, Gotanda, Peller, & Thomas, 1995; Harris, 1993; Gotanda, 1995) Lynn and Parker (2006) further explain,

> CRT advocates have pointed out the irony and the frustrating legal pace of meaningful reform that has eliminated blatant hateful expressions of rac-ism, yet, kept intact exclusionary relations of power as exemplified by the le-gal conservative backlash of the courts, legislative bodies, voters, etc., against special rights for racially marginalized groups. (p. 260)

In her book, *The New Jim Crow: Mass Incarceration in the Age of Colorblind-ness*, Michelle Alexander (2012) points out,

> What has changed since the collapse of Jim Crow has less to do with the basic structure of our society than with the language we use to justify it. In the era of color-blindness, it is no longer socially permissible to use race ex-plicitly as a justification for discrimination, exclusion, and social contempt. So we don't. Rather than rely on race, we use our criminal justice system to label people of color "criminals" and then engage in all the practices we supposedly left behind. (p. 2)

Indeed, racism is alive and well and our court system is thriving as a hub to replicate white-supremacist policies and practices under the cover of a "post-racial" reality. As Alexander explains, "A formally color-blind system" creates and recreates racial discrimination by demanding "that anyone who wants to challenge racial bias in the system offer, in advance, clear proof that the racial disparities are the product of intentional racial discrimination—i.e., the work of a bigot" (p. 103). Thus, patterns of unequal treatment by police in the courts are not enough to prove discrimination—absent the shouting of a racial slur (and even then) there seems to be no formal way to combat the racism in our communities and courts.

CRT pushes back against such practices and starts with the notion that racism is normal, not aberrant, in American society" (Delgado & Stefancic, 2000, p. xv). They continue,

> Because racism is an ingrained feature of our landscape, it looks ordinary and natural to persons in the culture. Formal equal opportunity rules and laws that insist in treating blacks and whites (for example) alike can thus remedy only the more extreme and shocking forms of injustice . . . It can do little about the business-as-usual forms of racism that people of color confront every day and that account for much misery, alienation, and despair. (p. xv)

Racism then is not limited to crude acts of white supremacy and violence, rather in a CRT lens, racism is "endemic in U.S. society, deeply ingrained legally, culturally, and even psychologically" (Tate, 1997, p. 234). Moving from the foundation of seeing racism as endemic and "normal" in U.S. society, CRT offers several additional unifying themes. These themes are helpful for both individual teachers and larger systems in moving from an understanding of racism as individual acts of meanness to seeing the larger systemic issues of racialized oppression. Though this book tends to focus upon the individual actions and development of teachers, this work must be done in tandem with an understanding of the systemic forms of racism that infect all of our major institutions.

One tenant of CRT that must be highlighted, is the insistence on the experiential knowledge of people of color is legitimate, appropriate, and critical to understanding, analyzing and teaching about racial subordination (Yosso, 2005). What right then do I as a white woman have in utilizing this work to disrupt whiteness and white supremacy? Frankly, the white frames of knowing and theoretical models offer little to push me to antiracism. CRT stands in sharp contrast to the miseducation I have received regarding race. It forces me to actively disrupt my white ways of knowing and understanding the world.

White frames of knowing endorse color-blind discourses, refuse to name white as a "race," focus on individual achievement with no notice of the interdependent nature of success, recognize racism only in overt forms (men with torches), adapt an ahistorical approach to understanding the structure of the United States, and see racial discrimination as largely something that the Civil Rights Movement "fixed" and refuse to name let alone disrupt the systemic white supremacy that has shaped and continues to shape this nation. One of the most powerful tenets of CRT is the challenge to such dominant ideology. Yosso (2005) writes, *CRT* "challenges White privilege and refutes the claims that educational institutions make toward objectivity, meritocracy, color-blindness, race neutrality and equal opportunity" (p. 73). In the following section, I examine the construction of whiteness and in doing so illustrate the crucial need for pushing against dominant ideology that allows for sustaining whiteness. In short, without CRT the calls for anti-racist practice throughout this book would readily replicate a shallow and dominant way of knowing the world. That said, simply reading and being influenced by CRT does not shield me from the influences of whiteness that have shaped my world as the following section illustrates.

The Story Continues: Imagining White Enacting Whiteness

> *Whiteness, of course, has always been more of a strategy than an ethnic nomenclature.*
> —Mat Johnson, *Pym*, 2011

The previous chapter illustrated how race grew out of racism. The racial category of white is the most dangerous because with it emerges whiteness. James Baldwin wrote,

> America became white—the people who, as they claim, "settled the country" became white—because of the necessity of denying the Black presence, and justifying the Black subjugation. No community can be based on such a principle—or in other words, no community can be established on a genocidal lie (as quoted in Roediger, 1998, p. 178)

Whiteness is an ideology that promotes white supremacy and the degradation of people of color. It reserves the right to exclude absolutely and arbitrarily for the sole purpose of replicating itself and ensuring domination (Harris, 1993). Whiteness functions to provide and ensure those who are deemed white unearned privilege, power, and access. Di'Angelo (2011) explains whiteness as a series of processes and practices

> rather than as a discrete entity (i.e., skin color alone). Whiteness is dynamic, relational, and operating at all times and on myriad levels. These processes

and practices include basic rights, values, beliefs, perspectives and experiences purported to be commonly shared by all but which are actually only consistently afforded to white people. (p. 56)

Gilborn (2005) asserts, "Critical scholarship on whiteness is not an assault on white people per se: it is an assault on the socially constructed and constantly reinforced power of white identifications and interests" (p. 488). It is an assault on the mythology of whiteness. For this reason, anti-racists and critical race scholars have said the only path is to abolish whiteness. Whites, even those who actively resist whiteness and see it for the violent ideology that it is, are granted advantages in a white supremacist system. In an earlier draft I wrote "benefit from a white supremacist system." However, to continue to feed whiteness ultimately damages and destroys all of us, albeit in drastically different ways. In the *Souls of White Folk*, W. E. B. Du Bois (1920/1998) points to the misery of being "imprisoned" by the "phantasy" of whiteness:

> Am I, in my blackness, the sole sufferer? I suffer. And yet, somehow, above the suffering, above the shackled anger that beats the bars, above the hurt that crazes there surges in me a vast pity—pity for a people imprisoned and enthralled, hampered and made miserable for such a cause, for such a phantasy!" (p. 187)

The fantasy he refers to is that of white men and women clinging to a notion that they are so different and so exceptional that an entire country should be built around the fallacy of whiteness. Despite this, I regularly have white college students and colleagues challenging me that they will lose if they give up on whiteness. Whiteness is an ideology built on violence and hate and sustained on the fear of whites losing power. One must ask as Baldwin (implied), what is the cost of sustaining such a "genocidal lie"? What is the cost of continuing to educate white students in a manner that leads them to openly fear refuting and resisting the deception and damage perpetrated by whiteness?

White Privilege

The day I met my son he was wearing a blaze orange mesh football jersey. A few weeks later I would learn that Jerry had been in foster care his whole life and that his caseworker was actively seeking adoptive parents. But it makes for a tidier story to say that I went home that day and told my husband, "I met our son today."

Fast forward a few months. We are seated in an office going over paperwork to become licensed foster-adoptive parents. We have signed forms, filled out questionnaires, and submitted letters of recommendation. We slide the material across the desk to the case manager. She stacks it neatly into a file and then begins to repeatedly take a pen cap on and off. She clears her throat, and says, "I'm really sorry about this. I'm sure it is all fine. This is just procedure but, you have to have a criminal background check and have to be fingerprinted." I was stunned. Not for the background check. Not for the fingerprinting. But for the fact that anyone would consider allowing a child to be adopted into a home in which the parents' backgrounds had not been checked! This was a 5-year-old boy! I had once been a reference for a family that wanted to adopt a cat! Why wouldn't we be subjected to the highest level of scrutiny imaginable? (I am an animal lover—more of the dog variety—but recognize that cats should have safe homes too.) The point of course is that *some* children in our society are treated as disposable.)

My son is African American. My husband and I are white. At the time we sought to adopt our son, I had been a teacher for a few years and was pursuing a graduate degree. My husband had two advanced degrees and was a principal at a local school. We are white, middle-classed, heterosexual, and educated. We looked the part. It was assumed that we would be fantastic parents. Further, our willingness to adopt a male "waiting" child (not an infant) of color put us in a rare and celebrated group. We were *good* white people doing a *good* thing.

It wasn't until we met Jerry's foster grandmother, the woman who had taken Jerry in when he was an infant, that our whiteness was named and rightfully questioned. Ms. Pearl leveled her gaze at me, "How do you feel about raising a Black child?" I began thanking her for asking the question before the caseworker cut me off and embarrassingly answered for me, "They will love Jerry just as much as you do." Of course, we would love him and already did. Of course, that wasn't what she was asking. In the years I knew Ms. Pearl, we eventually talked about her question, but on that day, it went unanswered.

White privilege is held in the assumption that we are "good people" and will be "good parents." It is carried on the whispered apologies of background checks and the rushing through of required paperwork. It is cemented in the heart-felt declarations from white family, neighbors, and friends that Jerry was "so lucky to have us."

I have no doubt that my son and I were meant to connect. He forever changed and enriched my life. However, white privilege allowed me to have access to my son in the first place. I am a mother as a result of white supremacist systems that label me as good before I have ever deserved such a proclamation and label my son as lucky to have found me without ever asking him if that was the case.

It was painful to write that last section. However, to run from my own privilege, to make it an academic exercise in which I write about other white people embracing whiteness and privilege, while doing little to unearth my own is to hide behind a racist mask. I do not regret becoming Jerry's mother. I do not regret having support in making that legally happen. But to do the ongoing personal work required of white anti-racists, to stand with my son as he faces racism, to dream of a more just world, I have to realize the reality of the multitude of privileges whiteness has granted me. Beyond that, I have to claim the places where my silence and inaction perpetuated my privilege. This requires daily work. Case in point, I wrote the section on white privilege and adoption and then stopped for the day. A day later I picked the work back up and was stunned by how I presented my complete lack of agency in this process. A critical reader would likely (and perhaps already did) recognize the ways in which I placed myself as a passive victim on the receiving end of white privilege.

Think about it. In the scene in which our caseworker apologized to us for the need for background checks, I express my outrage and shock at the idea of the apology in the first place. However, I express that in retrospect and in the retelling. I expressed that rage in the car on the way home that day. In the office I smiled politely, brushed off the apology, and signed the forms needed to keep the adoption moving forward. I did not point out the absurdity and the racism in the interaction. Likewise, I missed a key opportunity to disrupt white privilege when the caseworker interrupted me when Ms. Pearl asked the crucial question, "How do you feel about adopting a Black child?" I did not return to her question. I did not make the space for her to express her feelings and fears about her foster grandson who had grown up in Black families up to this point, being adopted into a white family. I was an invited guest in her home and I sat passively as she posed a crucially important question that mattered greatly in the life of a little boy she loved deeply.

In both cases I relied on what scholar Alice McIntyre (1997) has called "nice white talk." She defines white talk as

> talk that serves to insulate white people from examining their/our individual and collective role(s) in the perpetuation of racism. It is a result of whites talking uncritically with/to other whites, all the while resisting critique and massaging each other's racist attitudes, beliefs, and actions. (p. 45–46)

I examine these moments in my family's adoption story not to be persecuted or to wallow in guilt, nor to be lauded for my insight, but rather to illustrate the work it takes to challenge white privilege and the racialized socialization that I have consumed throughout my life in the United States.

Instead of continuing down this path, I follow in the footsteps of many fighting for racial justice and equity in schools and seek inclusive anti-racist multicultural education for *all* students. To do this effectively, teachers must be willing to examine their own biases. This is especially true of white teachers, who all too often have been socialized to view ourselves and our lives as neutral, as a holding place to compare all others and as the rubric determining which students and families are worthy and which fall outside the norm. CRT is one powerful tool to disrupt the myths of neutrality and color blindness that aid in supporting white supremacy.

CRT in Education

CRT was first introduced to the field of education by Gloria Ladson-Billings and William Tate in 1995 at the American Educational Researchers Association annual meeting. The talk, and later essay, explained how CRT was relevant to dismantling racial inequality in schools. In the article, Ladson-Billings and Tate assert three propositions:

1. Race continues to be a significant factor in determining inequity in the United States.
2. U.S. society is based on property rights.
3. The intersection of race and property rights creates an analytical tool through which we can understand social and, consequently, school inequity (p. 48).

Most specifically, the authors highlight legal scholar Cheryl Harris' (1993) work, "Whiteness as Property" and link it to education. In this seminal piece Harris argues that whiteness becomes a form of property because of the rights it affords those who are considered white. (These include the "property functions of whiteness," "the rights of disposition," "rights of use and enjoyment," and "absolute right to exclude.") Ladson-Billings and Tate (1995) connect this to understanding patterns of exclusion and inequity in schools in stating:

> In schooling the absolute right to exclude was demonstrated initially by denying blacks access to schooling altogether. Later, it was demonstrated by the creation and maintenance of separate schools. More recently it has been demonstrated by white flight and the growing insistence of vouchers, public

funding of private schools, and schools of choice. Within schools the absolute right to exclude is demonstrated by resegregation via tracking. (p. 60)

Ladson-Billings' and Tate's work has continued to examine how CRT could be used to examine curriculum, instruction, assessment, school funding, and desegregation in education. Since its introduction to the field of education, numerous scholars have utilized CRT to address the continuing issues of racial oppression in our schools as well as offering new takes on CRT.

As stated earlier, all of CRT in the United States is undergirded by an understanding of the endemic nature of racism to this country. CRT scholars utilize a variety of tenets for CRT, and I will not engage all of them here. However, there are crucial aspects of CRT that animate anti-racist work. These include challenges to "a historicism" (Matusda, Lawrence, Delgado, & Crenshaw, 1993) and color blindness (color evasiveness). Additionally, CRT's insistence on the "centrality of experiential knowledge" through the use of counter stories (stories, experiences, and other ways of knowing that disrupt the white supremacist narrative) is crucial to inclusive anti-racist work. Here I utilize examples from an unlikely place—high school theatre—as a way to illustrate how a CRT analysis is core to anti-racist work.

All the World's a Stage . . . Or is It?

To mount an all-black production of *Death of A Salesman* or any other play conceived for white actors as an investigation of the human condition through the specifics of white culture is to deny us our own humanity, our own history, and the need to make our own investigations from the cultural ground on which we stand as black Americans. It is an assault on our presence, our difficult but honorable history in America, and an insult to our intelligence, our playwrights, and our many and varied contributions to the society and the world at large.

—August Wilson, (1997)

Scenario 1

A white friend writes to me exclaiming about the "creative production" she just heard about in which all the characters in the play, *To Kill a Mockingbird*, are cast in reverse. Tom Robinson and Calpurnia are played by white actors while Atticus, Scout, Jem, and the notorious Mr. Bob Ewell are played by Black actors. She thought I might want to know since I was interested in race and this really "pushed some boundaries."

In this scenario the ahistorical nature of understanding race and racial relations is quite clear. In reversing the roles of the characters in *To Kill a Mockingbird*, the director is stating that history does not matter and specifically the racial subjugation of Blacks is insignificant and mutable. For those who have forgotten the story, Mayella Ewell is a poor white woman who falsely accuses Tom Robinson, a disabled Black man, of rape. The story is told through the eyes of a white character, Jean Louise Finch (Scout) as she looks back on her childhood. From her vantage point we see her father, Atticus, the white-lawyer-hero who takes Robinson's case even though he knows he will lose. (We never hear from Tom Robinson except in the oversimplified way that Scout protrays him.) Though story is set in the 1930s in the fictional Southern town of Maycomb, Alabama, and the author, Harper Lee, was clearly influenced by numerous real-life cases in which Black men and boys were accused of raping or otherwise defiling white women.

While it is true that Atticus, the white "hero" lawyer in the story stresses that "you never really understand a man until you walk in his shoes," the metaphor can only go so far. Despite so many white folks, myself included, wanting and needing a hero in the fictional Atticus, he too functions within a white supremacist model. He employs Calpurnia, a Black woman who cares for the children and is *almost* part of the family—but not really—she can't eat with them. He tells his daughter, Scout, that she shouldn't use the "N" word, because it is common—not because it is rooted in racial hate and degradation. He is often held up as an evolved character—even President Obama quoted him in his farewell speech, but Atticus is a white lawyer, working in a white supremacist system, at times agitating for change, at times not. The key is that his identity, his access, and his actions are rooted in whiteness. (This was true of Atticus long before the "sequel" *Go Set a Watchman* was released, perhaps without the author's permission, in 2015. Upon the release many white readers who had fallen in love with Atticus were appalled that he was seen and heard doing racist "things." For some, reading *To Kill a Mockingbird* through a critical race lens makes the sequel— whether it was intended for publication or not—less of a departure and more of an examination of the enmeshed nature of racism.)

To mount a race reversed production of *To Kill a Mockingbird* requires that everyone jettison the history of white supremacy in this country. It requires that the actors pretend that racism did not grow out of race. It requires ignoring how race was created to build and sustain white racial privilege. The devastating impact of claiming to erase race is compounded when one considers the ramifications of such a stance on the law, policy, and institutions.

One can only reboot and recast *To Kill a Mockingbird* under such a delusion. If race does not exist, racism can't exist and therefore policies, practices, and pedagogies to address racism are not needed. Gotanda (1995) indicates that within the color-blind ideal, racism and racists are limited to those individuals "who maintain irrational prejudices" against persons of color. If that were true, the multiple manifestations of institutional racism: from soaring incarceration rates of Black and Brown men and women, to substandard housing in communities of color, to subpar education provided to Black and Brown children would not exist. Instead we would have small clusters of unenlightened white folks saying hateful things, but wielding no power. Sadly, racism is much more than just an individual prejudice. We can see it most forcefully in Trump's policies and his cabinet, but the prevalence of racism is not new. But it might be easier to ignore race and pretend it doesn't exist. Doing so allows a variety of forms of racial subjugation to be explained away as isolated phenomena unconnected to the way this society uses the category of race to sort, select, and determine who wins and who loses (Gotanda, 1995).

My own experiences leading anti-racist workshops with white in-service and preservice teachers confirm what multiple studies have illustrated—a belief in color blindness (or claiming we are post-racial) is still very prevalent. In some ways, this is a logical way to avoid difficult discussions of race. If one denies the saliency of race, one does not have to confront or battle racism.

Many white teachers are willing to attribute inequities in schools and larger society to anything but race. During one break in an anti-racist professional development session, a white faculty member tried, for several minutes, to get me to admit that focusing on racism was truly the wrong approach. I had used Hurricane Katrina as an example of the ways institutional racism exists in the basest and material ways. He challenged me on this by stating, "Those people in New Orleans, it wasn't about race; it was about social class." My point is not to deny the intersection between race and class. The events surrounding Hurricane Katrina help to illustrate the ways racism and poverty are intertwined in this country. However, this teacher did not want to discuss the aspects of racism and instead wanted to focus solely on social class. We need to address both class disparity and racism. Why were poor Black people left to fend for themselves as the waters rose in New Orleans and Mississippi? Why were white women escorted out of the super ome as elderly Black people were left to die (Delpit, 2012)? But the dominant culture of whiteness has found ways to explain away continuing inequity without directly naming race. Avoiding these discussions and the action that must emerge from such discussion makes lasting change impossible.

Scenario 2

> A white student writes me an angry e-mail following my decision to produce August Wilson's play, *The Piano Lesson*, featuring an all-Black cast. In it he emphatically tells me, I've talked to numerous people (both black and white though that should hardly matter) and none of them have been amenable to the idea of playing up a particular race. No one wants to be reminded of differences beyond their control and no one wants the drama department to be anything but enjoyable, inclusive, and good training for actors. (Affolter, 2013). He sends this despite the fact that I am also simultaneously producing another play so that no one will be excluded.

I remember being struck by the word inclusive when I read this e-mail. It is a term used and misused and here it seems to imply that racial identity and history should not be noted. But in stepping back from this response and others like it, I can understand the ways that pretending to ignore race, racial identity, and racism (what many call color blindness and DisCrit scholars refer to as color evasive) can aid in creating a community while not questioning the modes of maintenance of that community. This complacency leads directly to a comforting belief in meritocracy—the idea that we all gain, we all lose, and we all have an equal chance to, in this case, participate in the theatre community, take whatever classes we choose, or achieve or not achieve in high school. In the student's e-mail and subsequent pushback by white cast members in the other play I realized how much whites rely on the myth of race neutrality and a belief in meritocracy—two key beliefs that CRT rejects.

The thinking goes like this, everyone should have a chance to be in any play that they audition for regardless of the role. This means that a play that explicitly calls for a Black actor because of the specific history of Blacks in the United States rooted to the play, could be played by anyone. Instead of taking into account both the historical and cultural reality of the play, white students were threatened. The central conflict of the play—the "lesson" within *The Piano Lesson*—revolves around the worth of people and property. The piano in question was originally "purchased" with one and a half slaves: the ancestors of the two main characters in the play, Boy Willie and Berniece. The family's history was eventually carved into the piano by the sibling's great-grandfather and Boy Willie and Berniece's father loses his life after stealing the piano. It now sits in Berniece's parlor in Pittsburgh. Boy Willie wants to sell the piano and use the money to buy the very land his family was enslaved on and Berniece contends that no amount of money can cover the cost and loss represented by the piano.

I offer the summary here to stress why the actors playing these roles *must* be African American. This is not a play that can ignore race. (And really can any play do that in our racialized country?) It is a play deeply rooted in America's original sin of slavery. Moreover, this is a story of a Black family—their story. This is not a universal story, but one rooted to the history, struggle, and survival of a family who did not matter in a white world. No white person appears in the play and (though whiteness in the form of the enmeshed nature of racism in the past and present of this family and notions of whiteness as property are everywhere) it is a play not told for or about white people. Certainly, white audience could learn and listen, but the story is not theirs to own. In writing against the erasure of race, particularly of Black identity, August Wilson (1997) states,

> We want you to see us. We are black and beautiful. We are not patrons of the linguist environment that has us as "unqualified, and violators of public regulations." We are not a menace to society. We are not ashamed. We have an honorable history in the world of men. We come from a long line of honorable people with complex codes of ethics and social discourse who devised myths and systems of cosmology and systems of economics, who were themselves part of a long social and political history. We are not ashamed and do not need you to be ashamed for us. (p. 499)

Wilson's insistence of seeing the gifts and talents of Black communities and his desire to tell those stories is one key example of the power of counter stories. Counter stories, rooted in the experiential knowledge of people of color are core to CRT and core to dismantling and challenging what some have called the "master script." Swartz (1992) writes,

> Master scripting silences multiple voices and perspectives, primarily legitimizing dominant white, upper-class male voicings as the standard knowledge students need to know. All other accounts and perspectives are omitted from the master script unless they can be disempowered through misrepresentation. (p. 341)

One such misrepresentation is seen in the first scenario above: in which the portrayal of a disabled Black man can be switched to have a white person play the role so that it is clear "we all experience injustice." This is an example of an attempt to realign the master script. Another misrepresentation is one that insists that a play about a Black family and their struggle as well as the legacy and teachings left by their enslaved ancestors can somehow ignore race. Counter stories amplify what was never silent and allow for a more complete and complex story to be told.

In the example of *The Piano Lesson* (and in countless other classroom and curricular battles), instead of considering how theatre and education in general continually celebrate white dominant narratives and use those as a stand in for "universal"—or looking at the history of whitewashing that takes place on stages across the country—some white students (and some white families) chose to focus on their perceived exclusion. By invoking "color blindness" white students and their families can construct a claim of unequal treatment, because one should not "notice" race (unless of course the noticing is not mentioned and benefits whites). I am reminded of Ta-Nehisi Coates' (2015) observation of watching white families overtake sidewalks as if they owned them. He writes, "I saw them lost in conversation with each other, mother and father, while their sons commanded entire sidewalks with their tricycles. The galaxy belonged to them, and as terror was communicated to our children, I saw mastery communicated to theirs" (p. 89).

The fog of hypocrisy in the white students and their families is so thick that one can get lost. But the notion here is that color blindness should hold in order to protect the rights, privileges, and access of white children. They can be excluded from nothing. Here we see, Harris's (1993) "property functions of whiteness" and "the absolute right to exclude." Laws and policies; curricula and schools; and even engagement or not with certain stories can only take place to the benefit of the dominant group, which often means exclusion of people of color.

Some of the most ardent fans of those who deny race or racism frequently misuse Dr. King's famous "not by the color of their skin but by the content of their character" as a shorthand way of showing that "not seeing race" is a progressive way around racism. (Conservatives have also picked up this refrain as a way to twist ideas saying that noticing race exacerbates whatever remnants of racism remain in this country.) One thought behind this notion is that race *shouldn't* matter so in pretending that one doesn't "see" race, one can work towards a world in which race *doesn't* matter. Teachers professing (or enacting) erasure of race do so at great cost to their students. Teachers are dismissing an important identity feature of students. The danger of ignoring race and racism by white teachers makes it nearly impossible to work against racist socialization and stereotypes.

CRT rejects these race-neutral and ahistorical concepts and pushes instead a theory deeply rooted in the racialized history of the United States and in the counter stories of people of color that experience this lived reality. Utilizing CRT in education helps me work towards inclusive anti-racist practice because it forces me to realize the ingrained nature of racism and works to name, expose, and change those patterns in our schools. (For personal exploration of theory in your own practice see Appendix C: "Fire in the Belly: An Exercise in Several Parts.")

Applying CRT in Anti-Racist Teaching

Anti-racist education specifically and actively challenges racism in education by examining racist school structures and policies and problematizing whiteness (Sleeter & Bernal Delgado, 2005). Additionally, anti-racist education seeks to understand the various ways that racism impacts the lived realities of people in overt and less visible ways. Anti-racist education centers diverse forms of knowledge and experiences and utilizes that knowledge to disrupt and challenge racial inequity (Pollack, 2008). Finally, anti-racist teaching requires continued self-reflection and learning. Kailin (2002) stresses this idea of teacher learning as a key element to anti-racist pedagogy. She writes,

> The assumption underlying antiracist pedagogy for teachers is that it is necessary for them to confront racism in their backgrounds and their backyards in order to become conscious of how it is expressed in their teaching practice and their interaction with students of color, as well as white students." (p. 18)

Once, during a first-round interview for an academic position, I was discussing anti-racist teaching when the interviewer stopped me and asserted, "I'm going to tell you right now that you are going to have to use a different term with our students. Anti-racist implies they might be racist and they just won't stand for that." When I replied that is exactly why such direct language is needed, the interviewer took great pains to tell me why I was incorrect, looked back at my CV, noted who I had studied with and said, "Oh, you are one of *those*..." This encounter reveals how much the term makes white people uncomfortable because the implication is that there is an active step (or several) that must be taken in order to embody anti-racism. It is not enough to avoid racial slurs and it is not enough to say, "I'm not racist." Much more is needed. Inclusive anti-racist work is complex and can often feel like the proverbial fog that Ms. Wilson references at the start of this book. Anti-racist work can be dense, all-encompassing, confusing, and isolating. To help dissipate some of the fog I offer some examples from a larger study I completed on anti-racist teachers. While each teacher I highlight here exhibits many of the qualities listed above, I will pull out some of the unique aspects of each teacher in an effort to move from abstract concepts to specific actions. I highlight two teachers of color and two white teachers in this section. The challenges and moments of celebration faced by anti-racist teachers of color and anti-racist white teachers are decidedly different. It is true that much of this text exhorts white teachers to engage in anti-racist practices and highlights what happens when they don't. It is also true that white people like myself are more often lauded within white groups for working against racism, as if we are going out of our way to do something good for "others." White people must take responsibility for racism (not call it something else or dismiss it) and must act to dismantle personal and systemic racism.

But there is a distinct danger in the discussion of anti-racism to ignore the work of people of color. They are often tasked with not only their own psychosocial well-being but also that of their students of color. From clubs, to mentoring, to coaching, to informal safe places students can go to in schools: teachers of color do crucial important work of helping students of color navigate the hostile racial environment of whiteness in schools. It's important to note that these teachers also have the same teaching load and expectations as their white peers, yet it is assumed they will do this extra caretaking work. It's not surprising then that teachers of color, particularly Black teachers are leaving the field and that only 7% of the teaching force is African American (Goldring, Taie, & Riddles, 2014).

I choose to include a few highlights of teachers of color working towards inclusive anti-racist classrooms to honor their expertise instead of minimizing or ignoring the work. Further, to lump that work under a rubric of anti-racist teacher, but only talk about white teachers gets us back to the same place we started—white supremacy at all costs. I am grateful for the many lessons I have received from colleagues of color and while whites cannot depend upon people of color to teach us, there are many spaces where if whites take the time to *listen* and be challenged—learning and positive change can take place.

Tracy Wilson

Tracy Wilson is quoted in the epigraph at the start of the book. She is a 45-year-old African American woman. She has been teaching for many years in a comprehensive public high school in a midsized city in the Midwest. Nearly half of the students at this school are students of color. Many of the students come from middle or working-class families. Ten of the roughly 130 teachers at this school are people of color.

Ms. Wilson's path to teaching started early in life when she and her siblings were some of the few African American students in a predominantly white community and school near the Rocky Mountains. Though her experiences in schools were varied, teachers that did not want to interact with or teach Black students typified her education. In one example, her second-grade teacher refused to use the term Negro (as was the accepted term of the day) but instead repeatedly used the word "nigra." She recalls a sixth grade teacher as the first teacher that "treated us like everyone else." She also credits her parents with informing the lessons she attempts to teach her students:

> They always had something positive to say about something that happened to you that wasn't even good. They would take that and turn it into a teaching lesson. I do that in my teaching. Kids come to me complaining about something that has happened I try to point out some growth, some change that has happened.

She continues to link the lessons she gained from watching her parents to the ways she works with students to battle the racism they face in schools. In the following example we hear Ms. Wilson explaining how she assists students of color with struggling against white supremacy and helping them find ways to challenge racism:

> Growing up in an all-white community I have seen things. You know when you are standing there watching a parent being insulted only because they are Black, not because of anything else and they kept their chin up and they always used that as a lesson. I did not like what I saw. I sometimes was angry and thinking, you got to stand up for yourself. And yet on the other hand, walked away thinking they had more courage standing up and keeping their face up instead of playing into what people were pushing them to play into. We get pushed quite often in terms of people pushing us to say, "show me your blackness." This is blackness that they have designed for us.

Part of Ms. Wilson's approach to anti-racist teaching involves risking her own psychological safety and well-being in an effort to understand and teach her students and her colleagues. Moule (2005) notes, "The psychological cost to the person of color (working for social justice) is high because retelling the stories that help students understand a different lived experience causes one to partially relive these experiences" (p. 28). I extend this argument to not simply reliving the stories but having some of the stories enacted repeatedly by colleagues, as was the case with Ms. Wilson.

Ms. Wilson also developed a strong sense of humor in the face of significant resistance to anti-racist work. In the following example she discusses a coping strategy she developed when encountering whites that denied the reality of racism:

I was once giving a presentation to a group and somebody raised their hand and said, "Why do Black people always have this chip on their shoulder?" I get that question a lot. What I did, I was ready for this comment and um, I thought what does a chip weigh and then multiply that times average instances that happen…and how old am I now? And I did all that calculation so when that comment came and this one woman said the comment…I said, "Frankly, I don't have a chip. If I look at my math I actually have a ranch style house sitting on my shoulder. That will weigh you down." (Laughs.) I was just tired of hearing that comment.

An additional hallmark of Ms. Wilson's teaching is her ability to get white students talking about the history of race and racism in this country without the students resorting to silence or recoiling in shame from their past. She seems to honor each student's humanity and dignity. bell hooks (2003) writes of her feelings around working with white students battling racism. She states,

> As a black teacher who works most often in predominantly white educational settings, I know that teaching students to unlearn racism is an affirmation of their essential goodness, or their humanity. When they are able to drop white supremacy and the quick-fix, phony sense of self-worth it brings them, they are able to discover their real worth as individuals able to face difference without fear. (p. 81)

Ms. Wilson still finds it important that students understand the long history of racism in this country, however she wants to avoid the "checking out" of whites from the conversation. She invites white students to examine the history of the United States but notes, "None of us were there during slavery." She explained that giving students that opening provided them with a way to then move to modern day manifestations of race. "I don't want them to stop because of guilt or use the "I wasn't there," excuse as a reason to not engage. So, I put it out there and it seems to give us space to move." In using this technique, Ms. Wilson is questioning whiteness while pushing her students to a broader understanding of systemic racism.

Ms. Wilson utilizes her own experiences as a Black woman to guide and teach students and colleagues about the real impact of racism. She also works to get white students to critique the privileges that come with being considered white while at the same time honoring their humanity. Additionally, she helps students of color find positive ways to challenge and stand up to racism.

Isabelle Kline

Ms. Kline is a 31-year-old white woman who has been teaching English for 8 years. Most recently she moved from teaching in a large, racially diverse high school in a midsized city in the Midwest (with nearly 50% of the population students of color) to teaching in a smaller, predominantly white suburban high school in the upper Midwest. In both settings Ms. Kline's teaching colleagues were/are predominantly white.

This change in teaching location helps illustrate the focus of the anti-racist teacher despite context. In her current teaching situation, her students come from predominantly white middle class backgrounds and over 90% of the high school graduates attend some sort of post-secondary institutions. Within this setting, she reports that students "blush and drop their voices when saying African American." Nonetheless, Ms. Kline's work is centered on dismantling white privilege and bringing to the fore marginalized voices. Though the approach to her work is different in a nearly all-white setting, her passion and commitment to the work does not change or waver.

Since she has been teaching in a nearly all-white setting, Ms. Kline has been in close e-mail contact with me regarding the types of struggles she faces regarding discussions of race, white privilege, and racism. For me, her stories illustrate both the need to do anti-racist work regardless of the racial demographics of the school and the ways that the work itself must be adapted to fit the needs of students in various settings. In the following example, Ms. Kline discusses work her white students did after reading two very different novels, both which deal with race in distinct ways. Ms. Kline chose to teach Mark Twain's "classic" text, *The Adventures of Huckleberry Finn*, the story of the boy, Huck, and a former slave, Jim (he is running away from his enslavement) and their adventures on the river as they escape from various tormentors. The book is a complicated study in race, racism, white supremacy, and power. The story is overlaid with the tension of two characters searching for various forms of freedom while a white boy (Huck) disrespects and rules over an adult Black man (Jim).

This book was contrasted with Zora Neale Hurston's (originally published in 1937) novel, *Their Eyes Were Watching God*. The novel tells the story of Janie, a Black woman, and her own quest for freedom, identity, dignity, and voice within various Black communities. The novels are striking in their differences: Who gets to tell the story? What versions of the world are revealed? The richness and complexity and potential risks in using such texts are revealed in the following comments:

The last day of class before break some of my 11th graders led the first class discussion of *Their Eyes Were Watching God.* They just finished essays on Huck Finn. They had to read a scholarly essay that interpreted the novel (Huck Finn) as racist or anti-racist, and then refute or agree with that scholar's interpretation. We had some incredibly heated discussions about white privilege. Kids were upset to see themselves as maybe engaging in a white fantasy of racial unity built on the devotion of a black man to a white child. They really wanted the novel to be anti-racist, and fought hard with words to articulate the humanity and satire. I felt satisfied that they were having conversations and struggles in their own minds that they'd never encountered. I was proud of the intellectual and emotional work they were doing.

Then, starting this new novel that has been my absolute favorite since I first read it half my life ago, something totally weird and unforeseen happened. After a good discussion about Janie and Nanny's visions of relationships and dreams, the student leaders announced that we'd play a game. The game was called "Talking Black." They would read a phrase in Standard English, and then two competing students would have to write that phrase in black dialect. I can believe that the intention was good.

We've read a bunch of works in dialect this year, and although they've talked about how it's difficult sometimes, and makes them read more slowly, they've never made any lame-ass remarks (like kids in my Talented and Gifted class at my old school did last year). But this "game" really pissed me off. It just seemed laced with triviality and disrespect.

So, I interrupted and got on my soapbox and talked about dialects as languages with conventions and structures just like any other language, and that dialect is realistic, not caricature, and that Zora Neale Hurston (1990) was an anthropologist and folklorist in addition to a novelist, so realistic voices were her intent, and so forth. The students nodded and said they understood, but I can't shake this image of white kids putting on black face and doing a minstrel dance in my classroom!

Ms. Kline's lifelong commitments to anti-racist work have pushed her to challenge issues in both all-white settings and multiracial settings. Certainly, she has had to engage in conversations differently in all white versus multiracial settings. However again, despite the differences in conversations and activities, Ms. Kline honors the importance of this work for *all* students. She also does not shy away from including material that forces students in all settings to meaningfully engage race, identity, power, privilege, and access.

Ms. Kline's work as an anti-racist teacher includes her own awareness of the visibility, power, and privilege afforded to her because she is white. In the following examples Ms. Kline focuses on two important aspects of anti-racist teaching; interrogation of her own place of power and privilege as a white teacher and assisting students with developing crucial skills to interrogate and change inequitable racial systems. Ms. Kline defines her work and explains how *ongoing* personal reflection coupled with action is key for those on that anti-racist path. She states,

> Teaching for social justice means helping students, schools, and communities recognize and combat inequities. I think one of my most important responsibilities, as a social justice educator is to confront white privilege in my classroom and in the school. I need to help myself, my colleagues, and my students understand how whiteness is normalized in society, to see the effects of privilege and to be equipped with the critical tools to question and counter this privilege.

Her focus on countering white privilege helps to illustrate yet another aspect of anti-racist teaching. Whites that work against racism must remember that they are part of a larger system of white dominance while simultaneously struggling against the ways that whiteness is enacted.

Ms. Kline's interrogations of whiteness led her to learn from others as well as consistently question her own positions and biases. She illustrates the importance aspect of the anti-racist teacher's self-reflection and self-interrogation:

> For example, when a student asks to use the restroom, do I consistently hand out hall passes, or do I do so only with students who I feel are more likely to be stopped in the hall? *Good communication means recognizing that my words and actions do send messages, even when I don't intend them to. I have to strive for awareness of the messages I am sending.* Good communication often involves advocating for students of color, and for other students who are disenfranchised in the school. This might mean vouching for a student in a situation in which she's being confronted by another staff member, or using my own privilege to lend credibility to a student's concern or point of view. Good communication also entails listening, even to those with whom I strongly disagree.

In the following comments we see Ms. Kline again interrogating her own position as a white woman and encouraging her students to reflect critically and challenge the assumptions made about them:

> Anti-racist teaching requires looking inward and outward. I have to engage in personal reflection. (What assumptions did I just make about three African American boys gathered outside the library?) Create opportunities for students to engage in personal reflection (When walking in the halls during class-time, are you stopped to show a hall pass? What do you notice about the ISS room?). And ensure that learning opportunities I create are made

up of diverse perspectives and voices and not just a "multicultural unit," but in their very essence.

Particularly striking in her self-interrogation is the focus on the needs of the students and the recognition of the relevance of these students' experiences in creating meaningful learning. Ms. Kline's curricular choices are key and will be discussed further in a later chapter.

Corrina Jameson

Ms. Jameson is a 38-year-old white woman who has been teaching for 15 years, "the majority of that time in California." She currently works as a migrant education teacher in a midsized mid-western city. Though she works with students throughout the city, her school "home base" is a small middle school in which 79% of the students are students of color. Within this school the majority of the teaching staff is white.

Ms. Jameson's work as an anti-racist teacher is an extension of the anti-racist work she was exposed to and involved in as a child. Though Ms. Jameson does not deny her white privilege and position, she feels her parents' approach to life exposed her to much more than the white dominant position:

> I grew up in low-income housing and my parents were civil rights workers in SNCC (Student Non-Violent Coordinating Committee). We always had multiracial and working-class friends and never felt we fit any one culture.

Ms. Jameson's father, whose story is featured prominently in a text on the civil rights movement, was killed when she was 13. That tragedy pushed Ms. Jameson to "carry on his traditions" and to seek ways to "learn more and more" about peace and social justice issues. Ms. Jameson's road to teaching was constantly interwoven with her social justice commitments. She worked in Central America during the Nicaraguan revolution and picked coffee. While there, she worked to link up Catholic parishes that practiced liberation theology.

Ms. Jameson began working with migrant education after she took a group of high school students to Mexico to work and stay in migrant shelters. From there she continued to advocate for students of migrant backgrounds:

> I went and worked at San Jose State University in a program that took migrant students who had made it to college and wanted to become bilingual teachers. It was an Ameri-corps type program. They stayed in college and

they were also making a commitment to become bilingual teachers. I did some preliminary teaching of just the basics of bilingual education with them and meanwhile I was teaching a course in bilingual education.

She sees her work as a teacher as a crucial way to carry out her dreams for a more just world. Though she currently works in migrant education at the middle school level, in the past, in addition to her university teaching, she has worked as both a Spanish and history teacher in high school and as a teacher's aide at the elementary level. Of her current students she states,

> My students are all on a path toward biculturalism. I see them as the great hope for a just society. It is bicultural people who COULD become the cultural translators that lift the goggles from the eyes of Euro-Americans so that they can see the souls of those they now erase—of those whose gifts are now invisible to them. I tell my students that they are the future friends, colleagues, life partners, doctors, healers, reporters, mail carriers, mechanics, and teachers of my own children. I tell them that the choices they make now will mean that either my grandchildren have a peaceful and just community or a violent, racist one.

Ms. Jameson's path as an anti-racist educator forces her to confront the way whiteness and white experiences stand in as the universal experience for all. She is anxious to push away that dominance so that her students may be seen and heard. Her work embodies anti-racist and culturally relevant pedagogy and will be discussed much more in the following chapter.

Ms. Jameson's work towards anti-racist social justice comes from early exposure to her parents' anti-racist activism. From the models provided to her as a child, Ms. Jameson has continued to develop many important attributes of the anti-racist teacher. She actively critiques the dominance of whiteness and works to bring her students' stories and experiences to the fore. She sees her students as her teachers and as important change makers in the world. Much of the power of Ms. Jameson's anti-racist teaching again stems from her willingness to make visible, through listening, the stories of her students' lives.

Alice Fuentes

Ms. Fuentes is a 45-year-old Latinx. Ms. Fuentes has spent her entire teaching career (13 years) in various alternative programs aimed at high school students who are not succeeding in a traditional high school setting. For many years Ms. Fuentes worked in an off campus program designed for teen mothers. She currently works in a school-within-a-school setting in a program that "targets students that are failing in their academic classes and have fallen behind on credits." Though this program is located in a high school that serves 2,000 students, Ms. Fuentes' program deliberately focuses on creating a smaller and separate environment.

Ms. Fuentes' sees her work in the classroom on very personal terms. Like Ms. Jameson, she sees the students as makers of meaning and attempts to work with them to help them see the impact they have on others:

> Teaching means change. It means giving somebody the tools, not only to be their own advocate, but also to recognize that their life means something; that your life impacts somebody. You are not an island; you are not alone, when you do something it has repercussions. That is why there is such a big responsibility in being human. . . . when I talk to the kids I talk about how your soul touches other souls. I am not talking about religion, because it is not religion. It is about what you do and how it impacts others. Unless you start living in that moment, you are not going to be somebody that is going to look inside and be productive. Not only because it is good to be productive, but because I know that my life matters and when I do something it impacts others.

Not surprisingly given the way Ms. Fuentes pushes her students to make connections to others' lives, she sees fighting racism as a key to understanding what social justice means:

> For me social justice is centered on the idea that we admit we live in a world that is colored by the mirror of race. Race, whether we like it or not here in the U.S., is covered under this fiction that we don't see it. In order for us to move forward in what we call the social agenda, helping others to better themselves, to get an education, anything, you have to admit that is the issue. And once you admit that there is an issue, then you can move forward in creating that change to happen.

Centralizing race is crucial to Ms. Fuentes' approach to nearly every lesson as the following comments illustrate:

> When we are doing any reading, race is always going to come up in the discussion. When kids are talking about personal problems, I say you know, within my culture, this is the way we approach these things. They look at me and say no, within my family. . . and I ask do you think this is the way in your family or is it because the culture dictates that this is the way we do it? I am always asking these questions. I just want to know. I don't know about your reality, and I want to know.

In Ms. Fuentes' comments we see the familiar refrain of the anti-racist teacher; valuing, honoring, and building meaning with students and connecting school to students' home culture. Also, in the above comments we see Ms. Fuentes refusal to assume she knows everything about students or their individual cultures.

Another important anti-racist refrain in Ms. Fuentes' approach to teaching is her absolute refusal to accept color-blind thinking:

> When we say things like, "When kids are in my room, I don't see color; I just see faces." When you say that you negate the reality of those students. To me, that is one of the most racist things you can say and they don't get it when I say it. I am very loving when they say it, but I tell them, "Look, when you say that you erase me, and you erase my reality." Nothing can happen then, nothing.

Though Ms. Fuentes joins her white anti-racist colleagues in resisting a color-blind approach, she also touches on a key way anti-racist teachers of color differ from their white colleagues. When she states, "You erase me and you erase my reality," she reminds me of the additional burden she must carry as a woman of color working against racism. While I would argue that none of the anti-racist teachers featured here see their struggle against racism at a distance, white anti-racist educators do have a protection that anti-racist teachers of color do not.

Ms. Fuentes' willingness to engage anti-racism and to challenge racist practices such as color-blind discourse carries with it dangers that anti-racist whites do not face. Ms. Fuentes' engagement in anti-racist work is a choice that she takes on because she believes it is important and crucial to teaching. Even though she experiences racism personally and regularly, she continues to engage the fight to transform schools into equitable anti-racist institutions for all students.

The Anti-Racist Teacher

Through offering the highlights of these anti-racist teachers, a working definition emerges. The anti-racist teachers offer counter stories to dominant versions of what education is or should be. All of the teachers profiled here are proud of the work they do. They frequently described their work as "important," "their passion," and "amazing." No one said, "I just teach." Instead they each attempted to paint a picture of the complexity, energy, and intellectual intensity required for teaching. By positively and professionally framing their work, these anti-racist educators offer an important counter story to what teaching can be. The framing of their work as positive and important is, I think, crucial to surviving in the often-hostile environment that anti-racist teachers frequently face.

All of the anti-racist teachers highlighted here came to teaching after making a conscious choice. None of the teachers in this study fell into teaching or followed a strictly traditional path on their way to teaching, though all went through formal university-based teacher education on their way to certification. All of the teachers came to teaching as a way to pursue a passion for some form of social justice. None of them see teaching as merely a job.

These teachers also offer an important counter story regarding their students. Again, all of the teachers highlighted here were quick to point out the strength and wisdom that resides in their students. They speak with joy of the energy they gain from their students. The high school teachers in particular were anxious to stress how much they learned from their students and how their students were "wonderful" and "insightful." Since most of these teachers work in racially diverse high schools, this overt praise was not accidental. They were anxious to counter the story of the "scary teenager" and in particular were interested in highlighting the achievements of their students of color. Again, instead of buying into the myths surrounding "urban teens" these teachers took the time to get to know their students and were anxious to spread a positive counter story regarding their students.

Coupled with the notion of promoting positive images of their students, these teachers spoke of making meaning with students in the classroom. None of the teachers in this study saw themselves as the sole keeper of knowledge in the classroom. Instead, they worked with students to help create the space where they all could share and learn from each other. All of these teachers worked to value and learn from students' home cultures and sought to make connections between a student's home and school.

The teachers in this study were also highly critical of white racial dominance in this world. Whether critiquing the global dominance of the United States, examining racial identity in literature, questioning the power of language in everyday school use, or studying history to understand the ramifications for racism today; each of these teachers centered race in their practice. In discussions with these teachers, it was clear that they did not shy away from difficult conversations regarding race and racism.

The white teachers profiled here did not avoid examining their own biases and positions of power. The white anti-racist teachers remained mindful that they too were part of a white supremacist system. These teachers worked to critique and question not only the larger systems, but also their own practices. Additionally, none of the teachers denied the importance of race and racism. Through discussing their work, it was clear that they were mindful of their students' lives. They did not ignore their students' racial identity. Instead, they found ways to acknowledge each student's identity and bring the gifts of that student and that student's family into the classroom. (For a close look at the fire in your belly: please see exercises listed in Appendix C.) In the following chapter, I work to bring notions of inclusion to anti-racist practice and specifically focus on one form of intersection frequently overlooked in racial justice work: disability.

3

Race, Disability, and Inclusion

We Have to Do This Together

We are the ones we have been waiting for . . .
—Alice Walker, 2006

Critical Race Theory (CRT) has provided a lens to understand the tenacity of whiteness and white supremacy. However, one area that still lags behind in many CRT discussions is the intersection of disability and race. In this chapter, I introduce the concept of DisCrit which combines critical disability studies with key concept of CRT. I do so to help illustrate crucial aspects of inclusive anti-racist work that are often overlooked if one only focuses on traditional notions "inclusion" or "anti-racist practice." As the title of the chapter suggests, as educators we must "do this together," and approach inclusive anti-racist work from an intersectional lens.

The avoidance or essentializing of disability by some CRT scholars may be rooted in the ways racial categories were used as a justification for deficit constructions of people of color. Take for example the history of eugenics and the ways the construction of whiteness has been used to classify those

Through the Fog, pages 45–66
Copyright © 2019 by Information Age Publishing

considered not white as less human and defective. Scholar Eli Clare (2017) writes, "The ableist invention of defectiveness functions as an indisputable justification . . . for many systems of oppression" (p. 23).

Consider the following example of ableism (a system that privileges those perceived to be "normal" or typical (without a disability or perceived disability) in action. Writing in 1851, Dr. Samuel Cartwright justified slavery because of imagined "disability" in African people. He writes, "It is this defective hematosis, or atmospherization of the blood, conjoined with a deficiency of cerebral manner in the cranium . . . which has rendered the people of Africa unable to take care of themselves" (as quoted in Clare, 2017, p. 24).

Cartwright goes on to invent various "mental disabilities" that he claims inflicted enslaved people. The most outrageous, "drapetomania," was "as much of disease of the mind as any other species of mental alienation." The main symptom of this "disease" was running away from slavery (Baynton, 2001, p. 38). Cartwright was hardly alone in his use of fictional disability to justify and support slavery. Others warned that the education of African Americans came "at the expense of the body, shortening the existence" and resulting in bodies "dwarfed or destroyed," by the effort of learning (Baynton, 2001, p. 38).

And the pattern of diagnosis and use of ableism to justify racism continues to this day. For example, though Black children represent only 17% of school enrollment, they represent 33% of those labeled "mentally retarded" (Erevelles & Minear, 2010). Black and Latinx students are also suspended and expelled at much higher rates than their white peers and more frequently are given the disability label of emotionally disturbed (Erevelles & Minear, 2010; Hoffman, 2014; Zion & Blanchette, 2011). All this, and more, are clear reasons why some critical race scholars and people of color in general might push away from associations with disability and disability rights. As Erevelles and Minear (2010) point out,

> The association of race with disability has been extremely detrimental to people of color in the U.S.—not just in education, but also historically where associations of race with disability have been used to justify the brutality of slavery, colonialism, and neo-colonialism. Unfortunately, rather than nurturing an alliance between race and disability, CRT scholars (like other radical scholars) have mistakenly conceived of disability as a biological category, as an immutable and pathological abnormality . . . (p. 132)

And disability scholars are not immune from running from such an alliance, either.

As Balcazar, Suarez-Balcazar, Taylor-Ritzler, and Keys (2010) reminds us,

> Persons of diverse racial backgrounds with disabilities have not been a primary focus of the disability movement, which has historically been populated largely by middle-class White people with disabilities... (p. 388)

But neither group can afford to ignore the other in the work of inclusive anti-racism. Further, the categories that render disability white or race—only belonging to people of color, entrench oppression and block attempts towards a more inclusive society. An individual is never simply a race, class, gender, or ability category. These and multiple other issues intertwine and are interdependent on one another. Cherrie Moraga writes, "The danger lies in ranking the oppressions. The danger lies in failing to acknowledge the specificity of oppression" (as quoted in Yosso, 2005, p. 73). In order to build a more inclusive world, we must take on the multiple forms of oppression that exist. I have already explained at some length the need to focus on race. Here I hope to push readers to understand how ableism functions to enable all sorts of oppression and offers racism a steroid-type boost to its potency.

One answer to the bifurcation of race from disability and disability from race comes in the form of "DisCrit." The theory, originally introduced by Subani Annamma and developed with colleagues David Connor and Beth Ferri (Annamma, Connor, & Ferri, 2013) offers a coherent and powerful expansion of CRT and moves towards a working theory for inclusive anti-racist practice.

Briefly, DisCrit asks us to consider "how race and dis/ability are built together in order to recognize the boundaries that only racism or ableism leave out..." (Connor, Ferri, & Annamma, 2016, p. 27). There are seven main tenets of DisCrit which I highlight here, each tenant however is explicated in much more length in the touchstone article by Annamma, Connor, and Ferri (2013).

First, DisCrit critiques notions of normalcy by "focusing on ways that forces of racism and ableism circulate interdependently." This relates to the *second tenet* which "values multidimensional identities" and rejects singular definitions of identity such as race *or* disability (Connor et al., 2016, p. 19). Like traditional CRT, the *third tenet* of DisCrit recognizes the social constructions of race and includes disability as a socially constructed category while rooting this to an understanding of the material and lived impact of being "labeled as raced or dis/abled..." (Connor et al., 2016). *Fourth,* DisCrit lifts up experiences and voices of marginalized populations within research. *Fifth,* DisCrit is rooted in the history and legal processes which have used race and disability to deny the rights of citizens. Linked to this, the *sixth* tenet of DisCrit expands notions of Whiteness as Property (Harris, 1993) to include conception of ability as property in order to examine how the construction of "normal" and "able" functions to chiefly benefit white, nondisabled, middle-class citizens.

And finally, just as CRT seeks to "eliminate racial oppression as part of the broader goal of ending all forms of oppression" (Dixson & Rousseau, 2006, p. 4), DisCrit "requires activism and supports all forms of resistance (Connor et al., 2016, p. 19). This final point is important in the context of this book and harkens back to my call to examine the one's "fire in the belly." It is never enough to simply theorize but as Connor and colleagues (2106) point out, "If theory can erase large portions of the population by ignoring their needs and realities, we also believe that theory can be emancipatory, offering oppressed groups a language of critique and resistance" (p. 26).

In thinking of how to apply DisCrit, particularly the interconnectedness of race and disability (along with multiple forms of identity) consider the following scenarios. First, I offer a summary of events described in Susan Burch and Hanna Joyner's (2007) book, *Unspeakable: The Junius Wilson Story*.

Language and Home—Found and Lost

Junius Wilson was born in 1908 in the predominantly African American community of Castle Haynes, North Carolina. At some point as a toddler, Junius became deaf. Facing the difficulties of raising a Black deaf child in poverty conditions in the Deep South, his mother sent Mr. Wilson to the North Carolina's residential school for the Colored Deaf and Blind in Raleigh, North Carolina. There he came in contact with his first and only Black deaf community. He learned what were known as Raleigh signs (signs that were unique to that institution and had no meaning outside the institution), learned to write his name but was not taught to read or write much else. In his teen years he was expelled for wandering away from a county fair and was returned home to Castle Haynes.

Mr. Wilson, now 17 years old, had no way of communicating with his hearing community. His behavior, such as touching people to get their attention, stamping his feet, or waving his arms, all acceptable modes of communication in deaf culture, was seen as dangerous in the Jim Crow South. Though the facts are now cloudy, Mr. Wilson was accused and found guilty of sexually assaulting a family friend. Charges against him were later dropped, but not until his life had been destroyed. The only reason Mr. Wilson likely lived at all after such an accusation was that the woman he allegedly assaulted was Black.

Mr. Wilson was placed in the North Carolina State Hospital for the Colored Insane. There, following eugenics protocol of the time, he was castrated and according to reports, "withdrew into himself... eyes downcast, silent, reserved... he gained a reputation as a gentle, childlike patient" (Burch & Joyner, 2007, p. 80). He also gave up any former deaf cultural habits like touching others to try to communicate.

Wilson's family, his father and his sister, located Mr. Wilson 21 years after his incarceration and sought to gain his release. His mother needed him to help her build a home and the family wanted him back in the community. Despite ample evidence that Mr. Wilson had not committed any crime, the state hospital refused to release him to his family.

During his decades of incarceration, Mr. Wilson met only two other people that recognized his gestures as Raleigh Signs. One was another "inmate" with whom Wilson had little contact until the end of his life. And another, a deaf Black man who a team of advocates connected to Wilson. The man, Everett Parker, though many years younger than Wilson, had attended the same segregated school for the deaf and blind and knew Raleigh signs. It is hard to imagine the relief that Wilson must have felt upon seeing someone sign to him and communicate to him as a fully functioning person. Burch and Joyner write (2007), "Shifting from ASL (American Sign Language) to Raleigh signs, Parker watched for recognition in Wilson's face. Wilson beamed" (p. 154). For the first time in 70 years or more, someone was speaking to him. And seeing him.

Wilson's incarceration continued despite charges being dropped sometime in the '70s and despite a push from a group of attorneys in Raleigh seeking to uphold the Civil Rights of Institutionalized Persons Act of 1980. In 1994, after many lawsuits and involvement of advocates, Junius Wilson was given a cottage on the grounds of the hospital. He died in 2001.

Junius Wilson was a Black man who was punished for being Black and deaf in a time when such differences were met with fear and punishment. His story is unique in the particularities of his situation, but not unique in the scope of the isolation and marginalization he endured. Consider the various aspects of Junius Wilson's life that were impacted by race, class, gender, disability, language, and education. His case is a study in exclusion at almost every turn. *Education*—What was offered to him and what was denied? What was he taught and what was assumed he wouldn't need? Mr. Wilson was taught Raleigh Sign and some vocational skills. He was not taught to read or write beyond his name, his mother's name, and his hometown. *Language*— How was his form of communication ultimately made obsolete because it was not a part of white deaf culture? *Gender*—How was a Black male teen, who had not yet learned the rules of "submission," seen as a threat in the Jim Crow South? How was his youth, race, and gender seen as justification for applying eugenic sterilization? *Class*—What recourse did a single Black mother living in poverty, who could not read or write, have in protecting her disabled child or in defending him in court? Why did the hospital turn his family away when they sought his release? What assumptions were made about his family, his ability to contribute to the community? His family's desire to have him as part of the community? All of these questions help bring to the fore the interconnected work of anti-racism and inclusion.

It might be tempting to place Wilson's story in the past as an example of the horrors of racism and ableism faced by African Americans in the Jim Crow South. Appalling to be sure, but not something that is particularly present today. But the intersection of race and disability and, in turn, racism and ableism, is alive and well today. In the following series of vignettes, I have deliberately omitted the names of the attackers and abusers and have included the names of the victims whenever possible. I do this because so much has already been taken from these individuals (in some cases their lives, and in all cases the sense that they are full people) that it seems appropriate to name them instead of the attackers.

He Was an Alcoholic

Seattle, Washington: John Williams, a First Nation woodcarver, was murdered by a police officer while walking down the street. Mr. Williams held a small legal-sized knife and a block of wood. Mr. Williams had severe hearing loss and was oblivious when the officer walked up behind him and ordered him to drop the knife. He kept walking, unaware of the officer behind him. Four seconds after the officer spoke, he shot Mr. Williams five times. In the subsequent investigation the officer described Williams as "very stern, very serious, having a very confrontational look on his face. He still had the knife out and [was in] a very confrontational posture" (Miletich, 2011, n.p.). The officer was eventually dismissed from the force, but was not charged with any crime.

In subsequent court proceedings and media coverage, significant emphasis was placed on Mr. William's struggle with alcohol and his "difficult life." And though alcoholism itself can be viewed as a form of disability, no effort was made to examine the role that ableism or racism played in the death of Mr. Williams. As Perry and Carter-Long (2016) indicate, "The fixation on alcohol and a difficult life obscures the fact that a police officer approached from behind a hard-of-hearing person walking peacefully down the street, gave verbal commands, and then shot him to death" (p. 19). Mr. Williams is part of a national pattern in which between one-third and one-half of all people killed by police are individuals with disabilities (Gardiner, Diaz, & Brown, 2016).

He Wasn't a Skilled Football Player

Dietrich, Idaho: In October 2015, three white male high school football players attacked their teammate, an 18-year-old, Black male reported to have mental disabilities. The three white men brutalized the Black teen by raping him with a wire coat hanger. The main attacker, who was charged as an adult, repeatedly taunted the victim in the weeks leading up to that attack—using the N-word, calling him "Kool-Aid," and "chicken eater," and forcing the victim to put a picture of a confederate flag on his computer and learn the words to a racist song (Miller, 2016). Some of the bullying prior to the assault was witnessed by coaches and other supervising adults. In the press coverage following the assault, the victim's father noted that one possible reason for ignoring the abuse directed at his son was the fact that his son was not a skilled football player in a town where football ruled supreme. Because of his disability, it was difficult for the victim to recall plays and he would be frequently called offsides (Johnson, 2016). Apparently, there is no room for mistakes in high school football and no room for difference. The main defendant was given no jail time for the attack and is likely to have his conviction dropped after completing community service.

The victim here is part of a larger trend of violence against disabled people. For example, according to a Justice Department report, people with disabilities between the ages of 16–19 are 2.5 times more likely to be victims of violent crimes compared to nondisabled peers. (Harrell, 2014). Further, though 46 states have hate crime laws on the books—17 of them do not list persons with disabilities as a protected group. So, in order to receive the dubious protection offered by hate crime laws one cannot be disabled, or at least should not introduce that as a factor in the crime committed against him or her. The point is that disability functions WITH other protected categories and yet is set aside as not important or worth noting.

It is a TOY TRUCK!

North Miami: In July of 2016, a 23-year old Afro-Latino man with autism, Arnaldo Rios-Santos, who was later described in the press as "nonverbal" and "relatively low functioning," wandered away from his group home. He carried a small toy truck. Charles Kinsey, a Black mental health worker at the facility, went to retrieve the young man who by then was sitting in the middle of a street. Police arrived at the scene, stating that they had received a 911 call saying an armed man was threatening suicide. Kinsey then laid flat on his back and put his hands in the air. The young man in his care remained sitting up nearby. Kinsey, hands still in the air, simultaneously tried to protect his client and himself as police guns were drawn. In a tape of the incident Kinsey tries to explain that no one is armed and that the young man with him only has a toy truck. "A toy truck . . . I am a behavior therapist at the group home" (Holpuch & Barton, 2016, n.p.). At other points in the recording, he is trying to convince the young man with autism to lie on his stomach. He does all of this with his arms in the air and flat on his back. He is seen lifting his head to communicate with the police and the young man in his care. The young man continues to play with the truck and does not respond to the events around him. He sits cross legged near Kinsey's feet. Neither man makes any move towards the police. Despite all of this and no one (except the police) armed, three shots were fired at Kinsey and the young man. One hit Kinsey in the leg; he was subsequently handcuffed and searched. The officer who shot later said he was aiming for the unarmed autistic man, not Kinsey. The head of the Miami-Dade Police Benevolent Association claimed the officer was trying to protect Kinsey but instead "ended up wounding the man he was trying to save" (Harris, Ovalle, & Rabin, 2016, n.p.). This leads to a few questions: Who needed to be saved? In all footage and reporting of the event we see a man sitting upright playing with a toy and at his feet a Black man lying flat on his back while shouting "he is holding a toy truck." Who was being saved? How did race and disability merge here and why was it thought appropriate to "save" a man's life by firing on him?

Not in Our Schools

The stories go beyond police force or bullying and criminal behavior of students. Discrimination and violence against students with disabilities takes place in our schools on both an individual and systemic level. Restraints and abuse of students with disabilities in schools was enough to garner a Senate report on this issue. It is difficult to understand the scope of the abuse but an overview includes

> an Arizona teacher used duct tape to restrain a second grader to a chair because she was getting up to sharpen her pencil too frequently. In December 2011, a Kentucky school district restrained a nine-year-old child with autism in a duffel bag as punishment. The child's mother witnessed him struggling inside the bag while a teacher's aide stood by and did nothing. In Indiana,

a teen was repeatedly left alone and isolated in an unmonitored room for hours at a time during January 2011. On one occasion, he was prevented from using the bathroom and urinated on the floor. As punishment for urinating he was secluded again in the same room the following day, where he screamed and banged on the door to be let out. When no one came to his aid, he attempted to hang himself. Thankfully, he survived. A sixteen-year-old boy with disabilities in New York did not. He died in April 2012 after being restrained facedown by at least four school staff members for allegedly refusing to leave a basketball court. (Health, Education, Labor, & Pensions, 2014, p. 6)

The problem of abuse against students with disabilities should alarm all teachers. For teachers working towards inclusive anti-racist practice there are additional layers of concern. For some time, researchers have illustrated that students of color are disproportionately identified as having disabilities. For example, according to Zion and Blanchett (2011),

Students' risk index for being labeled as having a disability and placed in special education is impacted by their race/ethnicity, as evidenced in the 28th Annual Report to Congress (U.S. Department of Education, 2009). For example, American Indian/Alaska Native students experience a risk of 13.7%, African American students 12.4%, White students 8.7%, Hispanic students 8.3%, and Asian/Pacific Islander students 4.6% of being labeled as having a disability. (p. 2192)

While the labels themselves are problematic and often misapplied, even more insidious is how the labels come to mean different and decidedly inequitable education for many students of color.

Four Different School Systems

Earlier I noted the huge discrepancies in the number of students of color being labeled with disabilities in schools. These numbers are more problematic when one considers how students with disability are treated within the school system. Blanchett (2006) notes, "white privilege and racism have resulted in at least four sub-systems of American public schooling..." (p. 25). First is a general education system for students who are predominantly white and without disabilities. These students tend to be exposed to rigorous high-quality curricula, are taught by highly educated teachers with teaching credentials in the subjects they teach, and have access to updated physical facilities that contain "perks" like computer and science labs.

Blanchett describes the second subsystem as a general education system primarily for students of color (particularly African American and Latina/o students). These students attend schools with a high teacher turnover and are often taught by uncertified teachers or teachers with emergency licenses. Students in this "subsystem" frequently have little access to high quality "college prep" curriculum or to quality physical space in which to learn, never mind computer or science labs.

The third subsystem is a special education system for students who are predominantly white and labeled with, or perceived to have, a disability. These students are likely to be included in the general education population and are less likely to be pulled out of classes (thus losing instructional time with their peers) for services (i.e., speech and language, physical therapy) or segregated in separate classrooms.

The final subsystem according to Blanchett is a special education system for students of color—a disproportionate number of whom are African American students. Within this system students

> tend to spend 60% or more of their school day in segregated special education placements, meaning they participate in general education classes for no more than 40% of their day and may spend their entire school day in separate classrooms or separate school from those attended by their nondisabled peers. (Blanchett, 2006, p. 25)

In addition to this going against the Individuals with Disabilities Education Act (IDEA) requiring students to be educated in the least restrictive environment, such discrepancies point to ways that racism and construction of what is "normal" influence the quality of education students receive. Perhaps of most concern to classroom level teachers is the fact that numerous studies have shown that the disproportionate number of students of color (particularly African American students, followed by Latinx students) can be traced to the teacher referral process (Skiba et al., 2008). Further, many referrals were related to behavior rather than concerns over academics. Finally, racial disproportionality in disability categories is concentrated in the so-called or soft disability categories such as mental retardation, emotional disturbance, or learning disabilities (Skiba et al., 2008). These disabilities require judgment and testing on the part of educators. Determinations of these labels is quite likely impacted by the position and worldview of the educators making these distinctions. Given that the United States is a wholly racialized society and that the largest percentage of teachers in the United States are white, this is an important point. Scholars, Gravios and Rosenfield (2006) noted that when schools used instructional consulting that supported teachers prior to the referral process, there were significantly decreased referrals and identifications for special education for all students (Skiba et al., 2008). This suggests that helping teachers reflect on their judgements and decisions can support both the teachers and students in making more equitable decisions for all students.

Critical race scholar, Donnor (2005) invites educators and others to interrogate the following:

> Who gets what (e.g., placement in advanced courses)? How and why do they get these advantages? Why did someone else or another group not receive the same benefits? Why does the same group continue to not benefit when all things are "equal"? Is this a historic pattern or an isolated case? (p. 62)

Clearly when it comes to race and disability—inequality and lack of access to quality educational opportunities are not isolated cases.

The inclusive anti-racist educator must grapple with these tensions. One cannot just see race or ignore race and focus on disability. We must move to inclusive education that encompasses much more.

We Have Those Inclusion Classrooms

In K–12 parlance, inclusion often means that students with identified disabilities receive their education in a regular education classroom (rather than being segregated in special education classrooms and separated from their nondisabled peers). (I want to expand the definition of inclusion to encompass much more than disability, but it is also important to examine how inclusion works for students with disabilities.) This version of inclusion is crucial for the basic civil rights of students with disabilities and stems from federal policy. As highlighted earlier in the chapter, students with disabilities are routinely educated in the most restrictive and least engaging environments. Even so, many schools will tell you they practice inclusion. Inclusion done badly is not inclusion at all, and can end up resegregating students with disabilities within regular education classes (if those classes are made available at all). The following section offers a few ideas of how to work against the ableism and racism found within many schools.

Least Dangerous Assumption

One very powerful mental shift that disrupt ableism racism involved in the education of students with disability is the concept of the "least dangerous assumption." Donnellan (1984) first introduced this concept to use when educational decisions were made "without conclusive information about a person's abilities or intelligence" (Jorgensen, Schuh, & Nisbet, 2006, p. 28). Jorgenson and colleagues continue, "...when working with individuals with significant disabilities...assume that they are competent because to do otherwise would result in fewer educational opportunities, omitted literacy instruction, a segregated education, and an adult life with fewer choices" (p. 28).

To operationalize this concept, consider this fictional scenario: a five-year-old Latinx student with significant physical and intellectual disabilities travels with her parents to enroll in kindergarten at her neighborhood school. This student does not verbally communicate and early tests indicate significant cognitive delays. Her parents insist that she understands both Spanish (the first language of her mother) and English (the first language of her father)—though they can offer no conclusive proof of this. They are confident that with appropriate supports she will benefit from learning in a regular education environment. The parents are particularly excited that the school has a bilingual program in Spanish and English and hope their daughter can be enrolled in the program. (In this school one must start the dual-language program in kindergarten.)

After meeting with the parents and the student, the school staff have a lengthy discussion whether it is appropriate to place this child in a regular education setting. Some staff are especially concerned with her "taking the place" of a "functioning child" in the bilingual program. Some staff argue that this child does not know much and will likely never learn much.

These professionals suggest the student be placed in a segregated multi-age classroom (though they don't use the term segregated) where she will be with children 5–12 years old. There she will be instructed in English-only and learn life skills such as dressing, cooking, and cleaning. As she ages activities will not match her age and she will likely be spoken to as if she is a small child. She might join her same age "regular peers" for lunch or special activities but most of her time she will be in her "special education wing."

Other staff at this fictitious meeting argue from the perspective of the least dangerous assumption. They suggest flipping the assumptions of deficit about the child. Instead, they suggest enrolling her in the program her parents requested. There teachers will attempt to teach her to read, write, and speak. They will support her with the accommodations she needs to access material. Perhaps they will look into forms of facilitated communications or other technology that might provide her ways to communicate with her teachers and peers. Her bilingual family is also included in the school community both for the support they offer all students in their child's class and for the wisdom they provide as to how to best to communicate. This child may never be able to fully communicate what she knows and does not know, but the least dangerous assumption moves away from a deficit model into a space that sees people with severe disabilities as competent and deserving of a high quality education. It forces decisions to be made in such a way that if one is wrong the *least dangerous* consequences result.

Moving Away from Deficit

But the least dangerous assumption is not the only tool needed to overcome some of the abelist and racist ideas blocking access for students of color in schools. As noted in earlier, students of color, particularly African American students are labeled with a disability at much higher rates than their white peers. This overrepresentation often leads to lower quality and less challenging education for students of color.

The overrepresentation is frequently a result of teachers working from a deficit model that sees racial and cultural differences as bad, wrong, and deficient. Researchers have long shown that teachers form ideas about students' academic abilities "based on interactions with students, rather than relying on analyses of their academic work" (Ahram, Fergus, & Noguera, 2011, p. 2245; see also Mehan, 1980; Rist, 1970). Ahram and colleagues (2011) continue, "Judgments teachers make about students are informed by their own perceptions of what they regard as appropriate classroom behavior. The cultural significance of these interpretations is inherent in both the formal and informal aspects of the assessment process…" (p. 2245). Thus, teachers can often see differences in behaviors and interactions among students that aren't part of the dominant culture as deficient, wrong, and in need of mediation.

Scholars Reid and Valle (2004) urge teachers to see students' differences and perhaps difficulties in school as "human variation rather than pathology…" (p. 473). To that end, one concrete step to moving against deficit constructions of students is to engage in creating a positive behavior profile for students, particularly students that challenge or frustrate teachers. (A detailed description of this exercise is available in the appendix.)

Armstrong (2000) suggested that teachers rethink the ways they describe students and move from deficit negative language to strengths. For example, instead of pathologizing a child with the term ADHD, Anderson offers that the child instead be described as a bodily kinesthetic learner; instead of labeling a child as impulsive consider seeing the strengths of the child's spontaneity.

To root this to "real life," and the work of anti-racism, I once again turn to our son, Jerry. When he was eight or nine, we received a call from the bus monitor saying that Jerry was behaving in a "menacing" manner. Upon further investigation we discovered that Jerry was making faces at another boy on the bus. The boy, a white friend from the neighborhood, was also engaged in the face making, but he was not labeled a threat (we learned this after talking to the boy's parents). Being silly or making faces, even mean faces, is developmentally appropriate for a 9-year-old. It is not menacing. And yet, when a Black male child does so the label moves from silliness to something much more sinister.

Causton and Tracy-Bronson (2015) invite educators to consider, "What would happen if all educators changed how they viewed and spoke about students? What if every student was viewed as a capable learner?" (p. 57). Instead of moving from deficit and allowing the racist and ableist socialization to define and label students, they urge teachers to consider the strengths a student brings and pause to note the ways our own perceptions may be distorting the gifts a child brings to the classroom. (For work on moving past deficit thinking please see exercises "But this student is..." and "Learning Profile" in Appendix D.)

Radical Inclusion (Isn't Radical)

While including students with disabilities in high quality general education classes with their peers is a crucial aspect to inclusive education, it is an incomplete definition of inclusion. In an attempt to expand the concept of inclusion, Bagileri, Bejoian, Broderick, Connor, and Valle (2011) offer that inclusion is

> (a) fundamentally about all learners (rather than just disabled learners), (b) is fundamentally about striving to make all learners' experiences with schooling inclusive and participatory rather than exclusionary and marginalizing (rather than just being concerned with where particular learners are physically placed), and (c) is concerned with aspirations for democratic and socially just education, and therefore fundamentally concerned with interrogating the cultural practices of schooling (rather than just seeking to prescribe procedural, techno-rational definitions of inclusive schooling to be implemented). (p. 2128)

This definition of inclusion is crucial for all educators to understand. It seems that inclusion has come to mean either something pertaining only to students with disabilities (in K–12 settings) or a watered-down vision of diversity in which all ideas are accepted and no vision of social justice or equity is promoted (college campuses). In the following section I seek to expand and clarify what inclusion can be by distilling a few "myths" surrounding the concept of inclusion.

The need for such clarity was made clear to me a few years ago when I was invited to speak at a college that was experiencing some struggles as the demographic shifted from a largely white, conservative base to a slightly more racially and ideologically diverse community. I was to talk about building inclusive learning communities. Unbeknownst to me, my session had been billed as one that would help professors connect with their more conservative students.

Just to be clear, it isn't only white conservatives that hold racist or other oppressive beliefs. However, what concerned me in the promotion of my session, and what I will attempt to clarify now, were the ways in which "inclusion" was being used as a way to protect students from being challenged when making racist or otherwise offensive remarks.

It is a myth to suggest that in order to practice inclusive pedagogy, all ideas must be validated and honored in the classroom. We are not the thought police, but as educators, we have a responsibility to help educate all of our students while ensuring that students from underrepresented communities are not unfairly targeted, silenced, or stereotyped. The term inclusion is being used more frequently in many educational settings. Inclusion misused in a broader definition means an inclusion that caters to *some* while saying *all* are welcome. It means a safe middle in which the status quo is inevitably rewarded. It has come to mean silencing some (most often those with historically marginalized identities) in order to make sure "all ideas" are honored. *Inclusion at its core must be about equity and justice.*

To get closer to a more encompassing definition of inclusion, it is crucial to be aware of the larger histories and diverse communities represented in our schools and beyond. Disrupting racism, ableism, homophobia, xenophobia, and other forms of oppression is crucial to building inclusive communities. This must happen while supporting students as they develop their own identity and understandings of who they are in the world. These ideas are not mutually exclusive.

Lately, I have listened with alarm as my colleagues claim that to be inclusive "we" must give all ideas equal weight within classroom discussions and campus activities. Under a large banner of "free speech," professors and pundits across the nation have shaken their heads in disdain as students and some faculty protest campus speakers that promote racism and other forms of oppression. We are told that we need to engage in civil discourse around these ideas, even when the platforms of such ideas are uncivil.

Students, many of whom face daily injustice and marginalization on predominantly white campuses, are being told they need to learn how to sit with discomfort and listen to both sides. But what if one side questions your very worth and presence on a college campus in the first place? Are you still obliged to listen? The other argument is that free speech is threatened when certain ideas are shut down. But what about speech of dissent? There are misguided legislative moves ironically called "Campus Free Speech Bills" springing up across the country. These bills seek to place serious sanctions on students engaging in a variety of free speech activities, including many forms of protest.

This is not inclusion. This is not free speech. This is a way for dominant views to go unquestioned, for white racial dominance to reassert itself and for those in the margins to be silenced and shamed. In the following section, I offer a few more examples of myths of inclusion and instead offer some alternatives that can lead to more radically inclusive (and anti-racist) classrooms.

Myths

Myth #1: *Inclusive pedagogy means all ideas are given the same airtime and all ideas are accepted without question.*

Providing students with a quality education means that we must push all students to resist a single or dominant story about the world. Therefore, some ideas need to be refuted and challenged. This can come in the form of wide-scale protest, or in more day to day interactions. When a student or colleague says something that is insensitive, may be a micro-aggression, or is perpetuating a variety of misinformation, there are ways to disrupt this without demeaning or shaming the person.

Ask the person to repeat or explain what they just said. Phrases like, "Can you say more about that?" can be helpful and offer the person a chance to explain what s/he means. Sometimes it helps to repeat back what you heard so that both the student and the rest of the class can pause to think about what was said. After that, it is important to make space for others in the class to challenge the idea. However, the teacher must not rely solely on other students to take up the challenge. There may be times when a statement is so outrageous that the teacher needs to directly address it without opening the floor for debate.

Frequently in discussions of education with white preservice or in-service teachers I encounter some form of deficit model thinking. Statements along the lines of, "Those parents don't seem to care about education as much as mine did"; "They come to school not ready to learn"; or "Those neighborhoods that these kids come from make it really hard to learn" are all fairly commonplace among white educators. Such comments are indicative of blaming communities of color for when our schools fail students of color. When such comments take place, it is important to be direct and concrete in pointing out the biases and socialization that underlie these statements. Helping students understand their own biases and supporting them as they critically think about the messages that are shaping their worlds is part of being an educator. Asking students, "What makes you think that?; "It sounds like you have some strong opinions about that issue"; "Can you tell us what in your experience led you to that conclusion?" can help further that self-reflection.

There tends to be a fear, at least in higher education, of making students feel bad, or attacking them for racist ideas. Often, I hear stories from students of color about some racist utterance made in class that was ignored by the professor. When students confront or query a professor about the issue, they are often told, "I am talking to the person during office hours." A private conversation may indeed be the best way to further the critical thinking of a given student. However, when white students' racist comments are left unquestioned in the classroom, the damage done to students of color in that class cannot be overlooked. Letting racist comments or comments that allow white to stand in as a universal slide by or deciding to talk about the issue to white students privately, sends a message that white students matter more than students of color. More specifically, it demonstrates that protecting white students' feelings is of paramount importance—important enough to ignore the needs of those that may be targeted by the racist remarks.

Asking questions, reframing what was said, inviting other ideas, and, yes, sometimes shutting down a comment are all crucial parts of working towards a more inclusive and racially just classroom community.

Myth #2: *Political correctness will impede the development of inclusive communities.*

It has become fashionable amongst policy makers of every persuasion to decry the notion of political correctness. The lazy thinking surrounding this attack is that we as a nation are having our free speech trampled on by insisting on "politically correct" language and discourse. We have a sitting president who regularly employs racist and xenophobic rhetoric, has publicly mocked a disabled man, utilizes racist fear-mongering, and traffics in white supremacy policy and actions.

Political correctness merely asks that we use words that don't demean another's humanity. This requires that we approach our learning with curiosity and that we recognize that people are experts on their own lives. Thus, if a transgender student asks that I use the plural pronouns "they" or "them" in reference to them, I need to honor the request. I also need to be willing to be corrected when I fail to use inclusive language.

Realizing that our words have power and history is crucial to the development of inclusive classrooms. Political correctness invites the growth and tension crucial for communities to be inclusive rather than assimilationist. People need words that empower, not belittle their identity, or that of others. Using such language strengthens our ability to speak and listen across power and difference in order to learn. Refusing to acknowledge that what we say matters and that the words we choose matter obscures the privilege and power, and rewards those already in dominant positions.

Myth #3: *An inclusive classroom means that everyone is comfortable at all times.*

This myth is closely related to the first myth. Building classroom communities that challenge dominant discourse and disrupt various forms of oppression requires all learners (including educators) to experience discomfort. Yes, everyone should feel physically safe in a classroom, but the expectation that everyone will feel comfortable is unreasonable and should be unwanted. Unfortunately, within white dominated classrooms, students of color are often not comfortable because of the celebration of whiteness and the multitudes of unexamined racial bias within the curricula and pedagogical practices. That form of discomfort should not continue. Instead, we must build classrooms in which we can interrogate the various ways we have been socialized to accept and promote various systems of dominance.

I once witnessed Geoff, a white male student teacher, handling such a moment perfectly. He began his social studies class with a series of film clips and headlines dealing with current world events. Earlier that week Major Nidal Hasan, a U.S. born citizen, opened fire at the Fort Hood, Texas army base, killing 13 people and wounding 32 others. News coverage highlighted that fact that Hasan was Muslim and the horrific event was soon labeled terrorism. When Geoff showed a picture of Hasan to his mostly white class, one of the students said, "Man, that guy just looks like a terrorist. They should have known he was going to do something like that." I saw other students nodding in agreement.

Geoff stopped the lesson. He asked the student directly why he thought that and asked the class if they agreed. What followed was a rich and sometimes uncomfortable conversation in which Geoff helped students see the ways that stereotypes and prejudice have shaped understanding and created Islamophobia. Geoff kept asking, "Can you tell someone is a terrorist by looking at them?" He asked students what they knew about Islam or the Middle East. He helped fill in some gaps in knowledge. And, he helped students begin to understand that their learning and information were partial at best.

I am reminded again of the importance of anti-racist education and disrupting such patterns of assumptions and misconceptions. Unfortunately, too many students have not had their assumptions and biases questioned because the adults around them are often unaware of their biases or if they are made aware of them, refuse to question them.

I was recently given a tangible example of this when one of my former students, informed me that she was struggling to find housing at Harvard (where she attended graduate school). Apparently, she had arranged to take the place of a young white woman who was leaving her apartment. Two days before she was set to move into her new place, she received a call from the girl saying that her roommates (all white) had seen her picture and had decided, "They just wouldn't be comfortable with living with someone like her." This student wears a hijab as part of her faith practice. The students rejecting her as a roommate attend one of the very best colleges in the world and yet their education to this point has not disrupted their biases or prejudice. Their education has done nothing to make them uncomfortable enough to reflect on their own narrow thinking. Discomfort has an important role, particularly for white students who have been taught to fear the "other" and told again and again they are normal and "right."

It is also the role of the teacher to notice patterns of communication within the classroom and be ready to disrupt such patterns (even if it causes discomfort). For example, in a study I conducted on experiences of students of color at predominantly white colleges, Mya, a Black woman, mentioned that in class she says something and then several moments later a white student will say a very similar thing and be rewarded and acknowledged for it. Instead of focusing on what a student may have repeated or ignored from a prior comment, a teacher can refocus on what was said earlier. For example, "That sounds a lot like what Mya said earlier. Mya do you want to expand on that point?" The teacher needs to be aware of which voices are privileged in the class. Who is afforded the most opportunity to speak? How much space is the teacher taking up in discussions? Being direct in the ways that we want students to communicate and inviting in a wider variety of viewpoints benefits everyone. Ultimately, when modeled well, students will take on this role and observe patterns of communication and point out areas of concern to the class.

> **Myth #4:** *One way to create an inclusive community is to declare on the first day of class, "This is a safe space."*

The concept of safe space is crucial and might be best known from work in LGBTQ communities. Activists and advocates realized students needed to know explicitly which professors, teachers, counselors, and other school staff they could approach to gain support and not hide their sexuality and or gender identity. LGBTQ adults and allies can place a symbol (often an inverted triangle in bright pink or rainbow colors sometimes with the words Safe Space superimposed) on their classroom or office doors. It is a short-hand way of offering support. But it is just a start.

My issue with naming a class or a workshop as a "safe space" at the very beginning is that it doesn't mean anything in the context of a new community. I have been to numerous social justice workshops where the facilitators assert, "This is a safe space," as a way to encourage people to participate and expect a group of strangers to embrace that as truth without really knowing what "safe" means.

This claim of safe space is compounded in the context of seeking inclusive racial justice within K–12 classrooms where there are a disproportionate number of nondisabled white women teachers. There, an announcement of safe space is rather ludicrous and somewhat egotistical. Essentially, white women are asking students of color to accept the classroom as a safe space because they say it is. It is an empty gesture and demands much more. There is risk in crossing racial lines and significant differences in power and access. And sometimes not crossing or not being a part is the safest form of self-care (particularly for students with marginalized identities). Declaring safe space requires humility and the realization that one learns from students. In order to do this a teacher must decenter the power in the room and make the space truly safe for more voices.

Rather than making a blanket statement of safe space, explain what the phrase means and ask students what they need to have in place for it to be safe for them. Then it is crucial that the teacher follow through on the parameters set in class. Students and teachers need to remind each other what it means to build a safe community throughout the class or workshop. Too often teachers declare a safe space and then it is never spoken about or addressed again.

Beyond gathering information about what safe space means, it is important to build a community within a class. Building ongoing opportunities for students to know one another, learn and use each other's names, listen to each other's experiences, and provide space for differing perspectives creates safe space. Safe space is not something that can be conjured without the work to back it up.

Myth #5: *Group work will cure it all.*

This myth is included in this book because I have seen far too many educators rely on "group work" when tackling issues of race and racism. While opportunities to engage in more personal discussion can be valuable, in order for the work to do more than increase racial divides and entrench racialized assumptions, students must have structure, modeling, and support. Effective discussions around race *require* that teachers take an active role and design multiple entry points for students to engage in the material. Reverting to poorly planned "group work" as a way to avoid leadership has more to with the educator's lack of training than it does quality pedagogy.

Consider this example. There is very popular activity in social justice workshops and classrooms that asks students to assess their own privilege. The activity can take a variety of formats, but generally speaking, participants are asked to stand on a line and take a step forward if a comment is true for them and backwards if a comment does not apply to them. The activity can be specifically tailored to a topic (like racism) or can address privilege more broadly. Statements might include: "I have never been stopped by the police and questioned because of my race"; "Most of my teachers looked like me and my family"; "If there is a problem I don't think twice about calling the police"; or "I can go shopping and be fairly certain I won't be followed in stores or harassed."

Recently a former student texted me and said, "Tell me how a professor led the 'step forward/step back activity' and then dismissed us without a debrief?" When the student asked the professor about this she was told that they would debrief next week. Next week came and went and the professor asked if anyone had strong opinions about the activity and when it was quiet, told students to get in groups and discuss what they felt. This is a prime example of abdicating responsibility in the face of discomfort. Group work, discussion starters, and activities that invite students to engage in difficult conversations are part of inclusive anti-racist work. However, the teacher *must* be prepared to lead, to offer observations, to make space for those who might be marginalized in such discussions, and to disrupt micro aggressions and misinformation. White people in particular are working against a lifetime of racist socialization. We cannot expect students to just know how to talk about issues and expect it is fine once they are face to face in small groups.

Myth #6: *If I do everything right, I will achieve inclusion.*

This may be frustrating to some. After all, isn't that the goal, to create inclusive spaces for all of our students? The point is that inclusion is a goal, just as anti-racism is a lens to continue to work against systems of oppression. Over the years I have participated in many triathlons and marathons. After each (especially after particularly challenging races) retrieving the finisher t-shirt and then later wearing the shirt (after showering) is a moment of pride and satisfaction. I finished the race. I claimed the prize. But anti-racism and inclusion doesn't work like that. There is no finish line. There is no t-shirt. Exclusion is present in every classroom. Teaching is a political act and, in that act, we make choices every day to include and exclude. The question isn't about how to avoid this. It is about honestly assessing what materials, activities, topics, pedagogical approaches, readings, and people one includes and excludes. It is about questioning one's assumption about who is capable and who is allowed to participate. The work is to confront one's own biases and move to making the most equitable decisions possible. The work requires being open enough to confront one's biases in order to be pushed when biases emerge and to continue to work towards the ideal. I refer to the epigraph, the title of an Alice Walker (2006) book, which tells us "we are the ones we have been waiting for." Confronting ableism, racism, and the multiple forms of oppression that shape education in the United States is difficult work. But it is work that educators can and must do. It is not work for a select few or for those that have some special calling. Instead it is the work of inclusive anti-racist teachers. Work that is the heart of teaching. Work that calls on each of us to look at what we do and how we do it and find a better way. (To explore aspects of inclusion and the impact on pedagogy see Appendix D: "Reflective Activities on Inclusive Practices.")

4

When the Teacher Doesn't Know

White Knowledge, White Teachers, White Community, White Explanations

The thing about it is that when I say to you, look, you have issues with race; you might be a racist person. It is not that you are a bad person. I think that is why people get uncomfortable, because then you are equating them with being a bad person. It is not about being a bad person, it is about this is your make up, these are the things you held onto you didn't know that you were. You can't escape it. What it is—is about self-reflection.

—Ms. Fuentes, high school teacher

In 1860, William J. Wilson, writing under the name "Ethiop," penned, "What Should we do with the White People?" (Roediger, 1998). In it he outlines the general path of genocide, dominance, and destruction that followed the arrival of white people in the new world. Given the behavior of whites in this country he rightfully asks, "Are they fit for self-government?" (p. 59). And he observes that they are "restless, grasping, unsaturated, they are ever on the lookout for not what is, or ought to be theirs, but for what they can get" (p. 59).

Through the Fog, pages 67–85
Copyright © 2019 by Information Age Publishing
67

In 2015, in his book, *Between the World and Me*, Ta-Nehisi Coates writes of people who consider themselves white and the ways they/we have tried to escape responsibility for replicating again and again racial systems of dominance and oppression—systems that privilege "The Dream," which celebrates and caters to whiteness while destroying those racial "others":

> No one directly proclaimed that schools were designed to sanctify failure and destruction. But a great number spoke of "personal responsibility" in a country authored and sustained by a criminal irresponsibility. The point of this language of "intention" and "personal responsibility" is broad exoneration. Mistakes were made. Bodies broken. People were enslaved. We meant well. We tried our best. "Good intention" is a hall pass through history, a sleeping pill that ensures The Dream. (p. 33)

These two authors, writing 155 years apart, have named what still plagues our country: racism—orchestrated, institutionalized, and canonized; forcing one to ask what *shall* we do with the white people? The answer has got to be radical change. This chapter examines the danger posed by white teachers who refuse to examine whiteness and disrupt its replication in their own practice.

Whites in the United States have continually found ways to take up space, use resources, arrange the world to their benefit, and then be offended, demand apologies, and/or exact retribution when this is pointed out to them. From sidewalks to classrooms to boardrooms to the nightly news to social media—space is taken up by white people who demand the right to be heard, to be seen, to take whatever they need to be comfortable and be forgiven when they take too much, break or make unjust laws, or say the wrong thing.

I recently witnessed whites taking space when I attended a Women's March in Montpelier, Vermont (one of the many that took place nationally on January 21, 2017). On the one hand, I was encouraged to see so many people pushing back against multiple forms of injustice; we are a small state, yet close to 15,000 people attended this march. I was pleased with the diverse lineup of speakers and was especially struck by the poetry of "Muslim Girls Making Change," a youth-led group of four young Muslim women of color. The group performed a few poems and ended with a solo poem about police violence against African Americans. The poem was raw and real and the poet connected the dots between Black children gunned down by police and the loss felt by their mothers, their families, and their communities.

The crowd cheered briefly following the poem, but the applause was cut short by an organizer, a white woman, followed by a parent, another white woman. These two said, "We have a lost child." Fine, in a large crowd no one would begrudge a parent looking for a child. The mother took the microphone and started calling the names of a pack of children that were hanging out together at the march and demanded they come forward. It was clear that these children were not in any real danger, as they were in a group, and quite possibly old enough to hang out with friends and give their parents the slip. But the mother held space at the microphone until someone in the crowd found the pack of wayward children; at which point, the mother then sternly said, "come to the front." The moment was over.

This is how white privilege is normalized. It is okay to step on the moment of a young poet of color who is speaking about the murder of Black children—what matters more is that white people feel comfortable. And so, a white mother is so secure in her right to take space that she centers her nonemergency and ignores or never notices how taking that space erased the student and minimized the message that Black Lives Matter.

This space taking is seen in the refrain "All Lives Matter," in reaction to the Black Lives Matter *movement*, ("All Lives Matter" is not a movement, it is a rhetorical reaction) as if noting the institutionally sanctioned violence being wielded against Black bodies, somehow diminishes the importance of whites. The expectations of taking space are heard in the endless stream of retroactive apologies that follow being "caught" for telling a racist joke, using a racist slur, dressing in Black face, using too much force in classroom discipline, utilizing draconian pedagogical approaches with Black and Brown children, allowing a predominantly Black city's water supply to be poisoned, ignoring the threat to Native land and water, or mistaking a toy gun for a real gun and gunning down a Black child. It is heard in the calls for and (celebration of) banning Muslims or Syrians or Mexicans or any other people deemed a "foreign" threat from our country. It is seen in the suspension and expulsion rates of Black and Brown students from our schools. It is heard in the cries of the racism of white college students and Supreme Court justices. It is embodied in a political climate that lauds politicians for "speaking their minds" when uttering bigotry. Daily we see the Trump administration injecting more hate and exclusion into our country through legislation and executive action. Giving up hope, or assuming someone else will "fix" this, is not an option for those on an inclusive antiracist path. For white teachers, teaching against this vein of selfishness and recognizing it in oneself is difficult and painful. But it is part of undoing the systemic racist system that is fed by whites with small and large acts of ignorance, violence, and neglect. Sustaining hope and demanding change in these times is difficult but necessary; it requires resisting the push to normalize xenophobia, racism, ableism, and misogyny and taking action.

Yes, We Can!

The night President Obama was first elected, my husband Steve and I cried tears of joy. Jerry, then a young teen laughed at us and then ran to the front door, threw it open and yelled to the street, "Yes, Obama!" We all stayed up late that night until the President and his family took the stage. The three of us silently stared at the screen. Steve and I cried some more. (And held our breath hoping that security was providing a force field to protect that beautiful family.) It was an important moment. Something had shifted in the world and it felt personal. Here on the screen was a Black man who had become President in a country that has never really dealt with its racist past. And this Black man had a white mother and white grandparents. It was a moment I didn't want to leave.

I flashed back to the day we adopted Jerry. His Black grandfather sat at breakfast with us, looking around the table saying, "I never thought I would see a day like this." He had experienced some of the worst forms of racial discrimination: from a white girl pulling her hand away in disgust when he tried to play a game with her as a young child, to facing vicious racism when he served in the military during World War II and being denied access to the benefits of the GI bill when he returned home from serving. This was a man white America consistently treated with hate and disdain. We were certainly a puzzle to him. And as he examined our newly formed family, I wonder what fears and hopes he held for his grandson and for us. So, too, as we watched President Obama and his family take the stage that night in Grant Park, we had fears and hopes. Many of them were oversized and many of them stemmed from our own refrain, "I never thought I would see a day like this."

The morning after President Obama's election, during my first hour class, when the National Anthem played (as it had done every morning since 9/11) one of my Black students (who never stood) stood up and put his hand over his heart. I stood up too. I usually sat quietly each morning while the anthem played. That day I stood. We smiled at each other and as he took his seat he said to me, "It's the first time I ever felt like standing up when that song came on." Me too.

I can't say that I really thought racism was going to end with the election of our first Black president. If anything, I worried that the pressure on President Obama to be both a symbol and a fixer of our racist society was too much and too great. But, I admit it gave me hope. I think I imbued the moment with more hope than it warranted because I am white. It was a chance for me to see something positive that whites had done alongside of people of color. I thought we had turned an important corner, and maybe we did for a moment, but, years later, as the news sunk in that our nation had elected a racist who traffics in misogyny, xenophobia, climate-change denial, ableism, who puts white supremacists in key positions, and praises neo-Nazis as "fine people," I realize that once again white folks would choose whiteness above all else, even as in the case of the over 50% of white women who voted for Trump, when it went against their own self-interest.

On the night of the election, CNN commentator, Van Jones, put it best when he described the election of Trump as a "white lash." Jones stated, "This is a white lash against a changing country. It is a white lash against a Black president in part." With those words Jones helped frame how resistant white America is to racial change. I don't blame the election of Donald Trump on President Obama, I blame white America for never dealing with the ways that white supremacy shaped and continues to shape our world. The current political reality requires much of all of us, especially white teachers working towards inclusive anti-racist practices. But good intentions are not enough, as seen in the following example.

Playing Slave Ship

White teachers can (often unknowingly) prop up a white supremacist regime. Once, when Jerry was 10, he came home from school quiet, refusing to play our trademark "soccer tag" or any of the usual after-school delights. As I was putting him to bed he told me that he was upset because the kids at school were playing "slave ship." In class that day the teacher had conducted a simulation of the Middle Passage. She turned the classroom tables upside down and had the children sit closely together to approximate the packed quarters of slave ships. The lesson had an impact, though it is doubtful that it was the one the teacher had intended. Later that day on the playground, the white students insisted the Black students climb on top of a play structure and stay there for the duration of recess. Jerry knew something about slavery in this country, and what was reinforced that day was that white folks controlled and demeaned Black folks then and now. (Of course, being forced to stay on top of a play structure for a 20-minute recess is not an approximation of slavery, but there is power in that moment to a Black child. Does he count? What is his history?)

I knew this teacher. I trusted her with my son and had no reason to believe that she had anything but the best of intentions in conducting this activity. I believe the teacher wanted to illustrate some of the material conditions that existed for enslaved people during the slave trade. It is important for young students to understand that enslaved people were taken by force from homes they knew and physically moved across an ocean. The teacher was attempting to expose students to the grim reality of the Middle Passage. But pieces were missing, such that students could take that lesson and turn it into a game. Certainly, some point of the lesson got through: white people controlling and containing Black people. But that was likely not the message the teacher had hoped the students understood.

What else might need to be in place for the simulation to work? Is it possible that an exercise like this simply is doomed to fail because it is impossible to fathom the inhumanity contained in the institution of slavery? Perhaps. But, hiding this country's original sin from students is also a way to preserve the white supremacy on which this country was founded and still benefits.

Instead, for this lesson to work there need to be several pre-steps. First, students need to have some concept of what being stolen and forced into slavery meant for an individual. It can be difficult for adults, let alone children, to conceive of the scale of human suffering represented by slavery.

I suggest starting by building from students' own lives. Ask students to draw or write about what home means to them and who is important to them. Ask students to make a list all of the things that make them feel comfortable and safe, and of the foods they associate with family. Students could also write their names and talk with one another, relating the story behind their names or nicknames.

Next, have students imagine that someone came to their home or to the place where they felt the most comfort and put everyone in chains and forced them outside. No one explained what was happening and the people in charge had whips and guns to take care and murdered anyone who tried to get away. Moms and Dads were split up. Children were taken from their mothers and fathers. (It is crucial for the teacher to be mindful of the different family stories in the class. For some students, particularly students from undocumented families, the fear of someone coming to the door and taking family members away to another country is not a historical exercise, but a daily fear and often a lived reality.) And then people were forced inside a huge ship, forced to lie down, and packed in as tightly as possible.

People were chained together and to walls and floor. They had little to eat or drink, just enough to keep as many as possible alive until they reached their destination on the other side of the ocean. The trip would have been horrible—and many people died in transit from disease, filthy conditions, and in some cases, people were killed when they tried to overthrow their captors. If you got sick, there was no one to clean up. There were no bathrooms so everyone had to lie in their own excrement. And whoever made it alive to North America (for slaves were also distributed in the Caribbean and South America) were sold to white landowners who didn't see them as people, but instead saw slaves as livestock and profit. These white slave owners did not speak the same language as the enslaved people; they changed everyone's names, and often split up families so children would never see their parents again. Children were banned from learning to read and write and were punished horribly if they were caught trying to do so. This is not a slave ship game. This is a human atrocity.

Of course, terrifying 10-year-olds with such gruesome details needs a deft touch. But moves such as playing slave ship or making mock-up posters of runaway slaves as part of a history project (which was done in 2017 in a New Jersey classroom) trivializes slavery and ignores that how brutal history.

Too often how "slavery" is taught damages Black students within these classrooms. It is important to be aware of who is in the room and how to balance the needs of everyone present. My point is, that in order to authentically teach about the foundations on which the country is built (and make no mistake, our country's history is rooted in genocide—of Native Americans and in the enslavement of Africans) one must think it through. It is difficult to do, perhaps too difficult for man.

This may be why a recent social studies textbook decided to deal with the institution of slavery by including it on a chapter on "immigrants," rather than confront a harsher reality. In the text, enslaved people are referred to as workers from Africa. The use of the term "workers" implies some compensation, some sense of dignity, some sense that people were not brought by force, stripped of home and family, and treated as less than human.

Perhaps, too, this is why a recent children's book, *A Birthday Cake for George Washington* (2016) was released and subsequently recalled after pressure from racial justice groups. The book portrayed happy enslaved people joyfully baking a birthday cake for the first president. If everyone was okay with the institution of slavery (look kids, "they" even baked birthday cakes!), then it must not be as horrible as some insist. It is a fallacy that children can't handle complex issues and thus must be protected (again who are we actually protecting?) My more cynical side says it is white adults who refuse to come to terms with the links between the legacy of slavery and the ramifications of slavery in today's world. To perpetuate such a myth is a miseducation for all of our students. In order to move on an inclusive anti-racist path, teachers must be willing to find out what they don't know. We must try to let all of our students know and understand the ways this country was built using slave labor. We must not be so worried about white children's feelings or about white guilt. Most days it seems that the only students hurt in the process of teaching our nation's history are those who are not white. (For activities that can deepen learning and disrupt racism see Appendix E: "Reflective Activities and Discussions of Race and Difference.")

Fast Twitch Muscles?

During his junior year, Jerry came home much earlier than normal. Before I could interrogate him about his school absence, he launched into his reasons. In a psychology class the teacher had given an attitude inventory regarding students' perceptions of sports. On the inventory one item read, "Some races are just better at sports than other races." Jerry told me, "No offense Mom, but I looked around the room and saw all those white people and knew how the discussion was going to go." As he had predicted, many white students said some "races" were better than others at sports, and some insisted that Black people had "fast twitch muscles" and thus were "naturally" better at sports. My son is a gifted athlete which made his frustration with the comments even more acute.

He tried to explain the social construct of race. He attempted to explain that race was a biological fallacy. Instead of his peers listening to him, they told him to "calm down." His white male classmates were particularly concerned when he challenged a white female classmate, as she asserted that Blacks were fundamentally genetically different than whites. When I asked how the teacher responded, Jerry told me, "He just said we should move on. I put my head on my desk and waited until the end of class and then I left." He then continued, "Mom, I don't think those teachers should talk about race; they don't know how to do it, so they just shouldn't."

There are several ways white racial dominance and oppression function in this example. Chief among them is how protecting white fragility was more important than attending to the damage done to my son in that moment. DiAngelo (2011) defines white fragility as "a state in which even a minimum amount of racial stress (felt by whites) becomes intolerable, triggering a range of defensive moves" (p. 54, parentheses mine). In this example, protecting the white female student who was positing racist ideas rooted in eugenics was the most important action in the room. The defensive moves included Jerry's white male peers telling him to calm down. The subtext of this could be summed up in: "It isn't a big deal to us, so it shouldn't be to you" and "we (as whites) are the arbiters of what is racist and what is not." The second defensive move was the silence and lack of direction by the teacher. In his silence he reinforced the racism in the room and protected the white students' feelings rather than considering the alienation and silencing of my son.

I actually had the artifact the students used. Listed among more typical items such as, "I like watching sports on television" or "Having sports in schools is a way to keep students involved in academics," was the offending item that read, "Some races are better at sports than other races."

I have little doubt that the teacher *intended* this inventory to be a way to spark discussion and determine where students stood on various issues. Such an inventory can be a useful way to start a unit and hook students into a lesson. It can inform the teacher of the ideas and interests in the room and allow him to tailor lessons to the needs of the class. The issue here is not that the inventory uncovered the racial stereotypes that were present in the class. Rather, the teacher made no effort to unpack the racism implicit in the statement itself or disrupt the myths surrounding such a statement.

For example, if the inventory were not changed at all and the statement still read, "Some races are better at sports than other races," the teacher needed to be prepared to meaningfully engage all responses. Thus, when someone offered, "Black people are faster because they have fast twitch muscles," the teacher needed to disrupt that misinformation and point out the racialized thinking that led to such a statement.

This includes explaining that race is a social construct and pointing out the false claims of biological difference. This includes engaging the class in a discussion of why the perception of Black athletes remains by asking about popular images of athletes and how those images are promoted and exploited.

It is important to understand that the education that needs to happen here is not for the sake of students of color in the room. (As in, "We only need to do this work if a Black student is present.") I do wish that my son had not been subjected to such a demeaning and alienating experience. But *he* already knew that the comments and ideas expressed that day were full of stereotypes and inaccuracies. The rest of the class left that day having their myths about race deepened, their racist ideology reinforced, their feelings protected, and their ability to talk about race even more limited. They learned again it was a controversial issue that needed to be avoided *especially* in the presence of people of color. They learned what was most important is that they, as the dominant group, be protected from any discomfort regarding race.

Some of Them Are Funny: Unlearning Racism

When we first moved to Vermont, Jerry joined the football team. He quickly made friends and soon enough our dining room was filled with hungry players (all white) devouring whatever food was available while attempting to complete homework. One night, Jerry excused himself to go shower. As soon as he was out of earshot one of the boys asked me, "Um, we sometimes tell racial jokes; is that okay to do? I mean we don't really mean it and some of them are funny." Luckily, I was in a teacher space that night (and less mama bear mode) and was able to get them to think about what made such jokes "funny." I also asked why they had asked me and not my son. The answer, "We don't want to make him mad, he's our friend." I ended with this statement, "I guess I can't really find those jokes funny when they make fun of entire people groups and are based on ugly stereotypes and often those jokes are aimed at people that are my family."

It might be easy to dismiss these young men as just examples of their rural upbringing. It is tempting perhaps, to place racists in a category of redneck or hillbilly as in, "of course *those* boys thought that." Those are the bad whites. Many of those of us who are white like to think of ourselves as good whites. (An idea I explore more completely in the closing chapter.) To engage in such thinking is to overlook the ways that all whites consume racist images and ideas daily. It is clear that within the vast majority of whites' education (not just rural white boys), there is a huge lack of racial awareness and knowledge. Fed on media and a current president who says inflammatory things about entire people groups (i.e., Mexicans are rapists) or uses coded language to defame communities of color by talking about the danger and decay of the "inner city," whites receive a distorted and dangerous picture of the racialized "other." It isn't just white boys or girls in rural towns.

These young men at the table were hungry to understand more about race and took baby steps in the short time I knew them in addressing their own racism. Future kitchen table conversations included the history of the N-word and why the Confederate flag is a racist emblem and not a symbol of pride. I feel fairly certain these conversations were among the first times any of them had been asked to think about race beyond jokes and racial slurs. Given more formal educational opportunities their understanding of race and racism (and their friendship with my son) would have gone much deeper.

White students need *all* teachers to be actively anti-racist or we simply continue to replicate white supremacy. It is that simple and that complex. When one strips away the recent horrors and insults hurled at children of color, we are left with a chilling reality that whites are being taught implicitly and unconsciously to devalue, disregard, degrade, and dismiss people of color. Black and Brown children in particular are targets of programs like "no excuse" schools in which shaming, controlling, and berating become the norm to help students "achieve." White parents would never allow this treatment for their white children. We cannot allow it for anyone's children. Unless we teach against this, we graduate another class of white students that perpetuate the same hate and another class of students of color who have been damaged by our educational system.

The trick is, of course, that white teachers have most often been taught in the same systems that celebrate white supremacy. The lucky ones come across teachers that help them disrupt patterns and begin to hone questions that lead them beyond a professed "color-evasiveness" and into a more critical stance against racism. Carefully reflecting on what we do and *why* within our classrooms is one key way to begin to practice the pedagogy needed to build and sustain inclusive and diverse campuses.

In order to create inclusive anti-racist spaces for all, white teachers must understand the difference between *intent* and *impact*. The psychology teacher did not (likely) intend to alienate my son or reinforce racist stereotypes with white students but the impact of that lesson (and the lack of facilitation) did just that. (For activities that can deepen learning and disrupt racism see Appendix E: "Reflective Activities and Discussions of Race and Difference.")

But What if We Are all White?

I guess we get away with a lot because we are so white, we don't have to address everything. We get away without the experience.

—Elaine Dunham, middle school teacher

When I moved to Vermont I was confronted with a new form of whiteness, one in which racism was purported to not be an issue because, "there are so few people of color here." I committed myself to finding ways to provide preservice and in-service teachers with the tools to meaningfully engage race, racial identity, and racism. The resistance to talking about race in nearly all-white settings was different from what I had encountered in more multiracial settings, but it was no less troubling.

One of my former students, Erika Berger, also became frustrated by the near absence of any discussions about race, power, and privilege in many rural classrooms. The two of us worked together to develop an independent research project in which she interviewed white teachers regarding their attitudes around teaching about race. *All* of our students must be given access to understanding the complexity of diversity in the United States and that must include a dynamic understanding of race. The case study described in the following section offers insight into teaching about race in predominantly white areas of the country where such topics have often been ignored.

In this study we set out to understand the levels of silence and avoidance of race in one school community. We found that the majority of the white teachers we spoke with were reluctant to talk about race in their classrooms and even uncomfortable in individual interviews with us. This is telling. How can we expect our students to grapple with the complexity of race in this country if many teachers do not have the fluidity or comfort with the topic? This is not meant as an indictment of these teachers, rather it is illustrative of the ways dominant education systems replicate themselves. Many of these teachers appear to have had limited opportunity within their own education and teacher training to meaningfully engage race.

Most often in our conversations with teachers, questions of race were ignored or avoided in favor of areas of relative familiarity: discussions of gender, sexuality, and socioeconomic status. Again, this is not to dismiss these issues. Rather, gender, sexuality, socioeconomic status (along with disability, which is rarely brought into discussions) exists *with* race. Race remains the primary way we award power, privilege, and access in this country. Of course, gender interacts with race and race interacts with disability and so on. I cannot divide myself into parts that are raced, classed, or disabled. Instead these pieces of my identity are intertwined. When we revert to discussions of race-less gender or class, we are once again promoting a white dominant view of things. The unmarked category of race becomes white and whiteness is reified and normalized.

Teachers in this study expressed that, given the largely white demographic in the local schools, discussions of race were waste of time. Again, white was not seen as a race and race only needed to be addressed if there were a critical mass of students of color. This argument was expressed in two ways. The first, talking about race, was a luxury that would ideally fit in the curriculum if time allowed. Iris Powers, an English teacher with over 20 years of experience, commented,

> If we weren't so busy it might be a nice idea to explore...you know maybe come up with some ideas. But the reality of being a teacher is that you are just kind of surviving, day by day, trying to get through curriculum, dealing with issues, so it is not something I have taken on.

While not wishing to dismiss the reality of limited time, these are *choices* made to justify absences in the curricula. Some issues are more important and thus "taking on" race is seen as a luxury or as an experience that white people don't need.

Further, in most of the interviews there was an underlying theme that white was not a race and thus, race in turn was not "an issue," in need of exploration. In this construction whites remain race-less and thus above "the experience" of race. (As if there is a single experience?) Additionally, there was a repetition that there were "no students of color" at any of the schools in the study, thus teachers felt no need to engage topics of race. Statements like "we are all white here," worked to erase the presence of students of color *that were in the very schools that the teachers were claiming were all white!*

Race, when discussed by the teachers at all, was clearly defined by a Black/white dichotomy in which Black was both negative and victimized and white was good and neutral. Take for example, the reaction of Mr. Bowman, a high school English teacher, when the interviewers asked why he thought students might resist discussions of race. He states, "No, no, it's not resistance, it's that they are tired of it. They know whites are good, Blacks are bad, or Blacks are the victims. They don't get a strong African American voice."

Ms. Watkins, a popular high school social studies teacher, also frames the Black/white dichotomy in expressing her concern for narrow notions of African American culture that her white students consume. She states,

> What they are taking from this is that they see Black culture as being about drugs and killing and wearing your pants below your butt. That is not what African American culture is. The kids would argue that they are admiring that culture by imitating it, but I feel they are mocking it.

Perhaps the narrower definition of race also led teachers to locate racism as a thing of the past. Gregg Mendenhall, a high school social studies teacher with 9 years of experience, remarked that discussing racism was, "I don't want to say pointless, because there are some places that are still racist, but our divide is more socioeconomic than racial."

Teachers in this study largely saw race as an issue of importance *if and only if* a significant number of students of color were physically present. This assertion is wrong on several fronts. The first is the premise on which the entire book rests, that is, that *all* students need to engage meaningfully with race. To deny white students access to the tools to effectively reflect on race, racial identity, and racism builds more walls of distortions between people groups; promotes an unnamed but ever-present state of false superiority whiteness; and denies white students opportunities to examine and explore their own racial identity. This, in turn, perpetuates racist ideology and allows for the institutionalized racism that frames our country to continue to go unquestioned and unnoticed by whites. Instead of creating educated citizens, we are miseducating all of our students and imbuing white students with false notions of superiority.

Another resistance to this claim rests on the rhetorical maneuver of naming a community as all white and assuming that whiteness is normal and has always been that way. This serves the purpose of simultaneously erasing both the history and present reality of people of color in a region. For example, the Abenaki Nation, a Native people populating the Northeast predates the arrival of the first European settlers by several hundred years (and archeological proof indicates Native people on this land as early as 10,000 BC). Recent U.S. census data show more than 3,000 Abenaki currently living in the region where our study was conducted (Moody, n.d.). And yet, to hear the teachers talk, there is no need to discuss racial or ethnic heritage because the town, community, and state are "all-white." The decoupling of the history of this region from the Abenaki is just one way in which whiteness results in an ahistorical understanding of the region. It prevents white students from making direct connections to the land and the interconnected history of their lives and the lives of people of color.

In addition to Native peoples, there is a direct and daily presence of people of color in many communities within this study due, in part, to reliance on migrant labor. Many white students who attend schools in this study live and work on dairy farms that employ Latinx migrant workers and their families. Again, when teachers insist on defining a community and a school as all white even in the face of *students in their classrooms*, they are missing a rich opportunity to connect students across difference and to highlight the interdependent nature of various communities.

Finally, as I alluded to earlier, students of color *are* in the very classrooms that teachers are claiming are all white. Though the schools that were represented by the teachers in this study were predominantly white, *none* of the schools were all white and *none* of the schools had just one student of color. This means that for those students who are not considered white (and thereby represent the marked category "race") their presence at the schools is simultaneously noticed and ignored.

I must challenge this reliance on the physical presence of students of color to regulate stereotypes or determine if race needs to be engaged in schools. In predominantly white settings with few students of color, teachers need to carefully consider the burden they are placing on students of color to "set the record straight" on issues of race. Placing students of color in the position of being the sole arbiters of racial consciousness and correctness for their white peers forces an unfair and unrealistic burden upon them. In this situation, students who are rarely acknowledged for their racial identity are asked to suddenly speak for all those in his or her perceived racial group. Instead, if as the teachers in this study noted, there is no "African American voice," students and teachers need materials that deal with African American history, literature, and music to provide students with a more nuanced view. In such a setting an African American student *may* feel inspired to share how the material *may* connect with his or her lived experience, or may not. In either case, the class and the teacher are not looking to the student as the sole arbiter of an entire group's experience.

If, however, race is synonymous with racism towards Blacks and racism is a thing of the past, there is no need to change the curriculum, explore racial identity, name white as a race, or discuss racism. If the only reason to examine race is to be able to study racism, Mr. Mendenhall reasoned, there was no need to examine one's own racial identity or help students' explore their own racial identity. Beverly Tatum (2007) is helpful in casting how this approach is damaging for all. She writes, "In a race-conscious society the development of a positive sense of racial or ethnic identity, not based on assumed superiority or inferiority is an important task for everyone" (p. 36).

One of the tasks then is to provide models for white teachers to explore their own identity while realizing that meaningfully engaging with race is an important task in all settings, regardless of the racial makeup of a particular school. There are some of exercises listed in the appendix that can be used as a starting point for such reflection.

In addition to self-reflection, all teachers need support in identifying and disrupting microaggressions and other oppressive acts when they occur. I bristle when white people say something along the lines of "What should white people do?" when confronted with examples of white privilege and dominance. Often this question is directed to a person of color as if the answers and the power to change systems of white racial dominance were held in a password protected vault that only people of color could open.

If *they* just told *us* what to do, *we* would do it. This is ludicrous because it suggests that white people have been unknowingly setting up and replicating systems that privilege whites and if *we only knew we would change*. History and current reality suggest otherwise. Nonetheless, as I have suggested time and again in this book, living in the United States means we consume racialized and racist images with our morning oatmeal. Thus, unlearning these messages and learning how to disrupt microaggressions is important work.

Personal Assessment

In order to move towards inclusive anti-racist practices, I suggest educators conduct a personal assessment of their classes and themselves. This consists of a series of questions that allow a teacher to consider the spaces of exclusion in their classrooms, campuses, and communities.

First, one should consider the classroom, campus, or community in which one works and ask: *Who is not here? Why?*

In this question I am not referring to daily attendance (though that might be something to consider if one notices patterns of absence). I am referring to the built-in exclusion that happens in educational settings across the country.

Currently in my work, I need to consider who has access via physical access, financial support, and educational background to be included at my college. And beyond that, I need to ask myself *why* and what systems are in place to give or deny access to a college education. No, I alone cannot combat these systems, but I also cannot ignore my role in promoting exclusion or encouraging a more inclusive classroom and campus whenever possible.

At the K–12 level this means examining classroom communities and schools in multiple ways.

- Who has access to the most rigorous and high-quality courses?
- How are reading groups set up?
- What happens to students with disabilities?
- Who is not here? Why?
- Who is invited into class?
- What types of learning, knowledge, communication styles, and classrooms are most valued and rewarded?

How do you determine what is included in a course? In some settings the freedom to choose materials is conscripted by local and state parameters, but even in such settings teachers have at least some freedom to determine how to approach material and which types of engagement will be rewarded. Sharing with students the goals of the course and why those are the chosen goals of the course can help demystify what is happening and can help students more readily understand the direction of the course.

Young children pick up on what is valued or not in a class. If they only see, for example, white characters in stories or hear histories that relate only to white people, they learn that is what is most important. If they constantly see Black and Brown children punished, all children learn that those children are the bad children.

Since leaving the high school classroom, I have made a point to volunteer and use my summers to teach in elementary schools in various communities. Once I was working with a group of kindergartners and I praised "Bryan," one of the Black students in the class for asking a great question about a story we had just read. After that he helped me find something in the classroom and did some other praise worthy task. I told him, "Bryan you are on fire today! Thanks for working so hard." At that point one of the white girls in the group told me, "He's usually bad. He usually has bad days and gets in trouble." I told her, "We all have bad days." She asserted, "Not me. I never get in trouble."

The teacher in this class is dedicated and works hard to include everyone. But we need to ask again, "*What is rewarded and what messages do we send when we sanction some and uplift others?*" Pausing to ask what we as educators value and how that plays out in our classrooms is an important step towards a more inclusive community.

This includes a closer inspection of the varying ways students are invited to engage in class. K–12 teachers are often masters at mixing things up and finding a variety of entry points for students to learn. Even so, it is worth reflecting upon what counts as participation and engagement in class. Check to see if you are falling into the trap of what one of my colleagues calls "spokes in a wheel." This is the format in which the teacher asks a question, one student answers it, the teacher responds in some way and then asks another question. In this setting, the educator remains the center of all conversation. Students are rewarded for their ability to engage in a large setting solely with the teacher instead of his peers. In such an example, students learn that listening to others' opinions and valuing the ideas of their peers is not nearly as crucial as being recognized by the teacher.

And this leads to the next question: "*Do you (as a teacher) realize that risks of engaging in difficult conversations (such as conversations about race) are not the same for all students?*" When students of color engage in discussions of race and racism in classes they often risk their own psychosocial safety. This is particularly true in predominantly white settings with white teachers. As I touched on earlier, it is crucial that we have real discussion and begin to break down the miseducation of whites in this country. It is also crucial that such discussions are done in a way that honor the diversity of experiences and the differing levels of vulnerability required in such discussions. Students of color are not delicate flowers in need of some paternalistic protection. However, to march through discussions without thinking through the implications for all in the class can result in exclusion and isolation to students that are already marginalized.

Finally, in terms of exclusion versus inclusion, it is important to ask: *How are your understandings of the world shaped and limited by your own socialization and education? What is your ongoing work in order to move towards being an inclusive anti-racist educator?* This work includes looking at one's own origin stories on race, disability, gender, class, and sexuality, and confronting the biases, contradictions, and tensions encountered regarding difference, diversity, equity, and access.

Rechecking Our Stories

This work does not require that one is perfect but it does require that one reflects on mistakes and considers the cost of the mistakes to students. For example, I was once talking to a class about inaccessible college campuses. A white male student athlete raised his hand and said he thought it was ridiculous to expect that *all* people should have access to a given campus. Behind these comments lie the socialization that celebrates fit and nondisabled bodies that can move in typical ways and access spaces that are designed exclusively for nondisabled people. In his mind, there was nothing wrong with that form of systematic exclusion.

I was angry when the student said this. I repeated back his words several times with increasing disgust and volume then proceeded to ask, "Who gets to make the decision of who should have access and who should not?" He then stammered out, "Oh, you were talking about like, people in wheelchairs. I thought you just meant like fat people on scooters." At that point I was too frustrated to continue. In my anger at the suggestion of being okay with systemic exclusion, I failed to engage the student. The rest of the class was left thinking that I was fine with discriminating against fat bodies. After all *those* people shouldn't expect to be included.

I am a passionate educator and reject the assertions that emotions are anti-intellectual. My mistake here was not expressing my frustration; it was allowing oppression to go unremarked upon. I don't recall if there was a student in the class that was atypical in terms of size. I do know that my silence stemmed from my own bias, my own story, and my own socialization that smaller and leaner is better. Working towards inclusive spaces requires pausing, disrupting the status quo of oppressive acts whenever possible, and noting when one fails or chooses to ignore. Privilege is the ability to ignore and benefit from oppression.

In his text "Letter from a Birmingham Jail" Dr. Martin Luther King Jr. (1963) famously wrote, "injustice anywhere is a threat to justice everywhere." But beyond this well know phrase is text which points to the reasons we push the need for all of us to engage across difference. He continues, "We are caught in an inescapable network of mutuality, tied in a single garment of destiny. What affects one directly, affects us all indirectly" (n.p.). This notion pushes one to see the interconnectedness of all of us. It frames my reasons for insisting that assisting students to meaningfully engage with race is a crucial task for all educators. In our highly racialized society to ignore difficult discussions around race deepens divisions and moves us further from recognizing our interconnectedness to those different from ourselves.

Religion scholar, David Anderson (2006) has written for the need for a "theology of interdependence," in which notions of false superiority and inferiority are eliminated in favor of a vision of more inclusive world. He quotes from a disability rights activist to help sum up the core points of this "theology of interdependence":

> Until we realize that we belong to a common humanity, that we all need each other, that we can help each other, we will continue to hide behind feelings of elitism and superiority and behind the walls of prejudice, judgment, and disdain that those feelings engender. (Jean Vanier, as quoted in Anderson, p. 50)

This is core to inclusive anti-racist education. To do so requires educators to examine their pedagogy as well as the curricular choices—which are discussed in the next chapter.

5

Yes, That's Me

Room for Myself

From the beginning,
Their words helped me like myself.
They gave me reasons—a certain shape and direction—
For the way that I was.
In the spaces between lines, punctuation, and stanzas,
I found room for myself,
A place where
My daydreams and doodles
Were not cause for reprimand,
Eye rolls, or exasperated laughs from teachers,
As they wondered why I *just couldn't pay attention*—
But instead, were possibilities.
In the stride of Maya Angelou's step,
Flash of her teeth,

Through the Fog, pages 87–108
Copyright © 2019 by Information Age Publishing
All rights of reproduction in any form reserved.

Joy of her feet,

I learned to find grace

In my own too-broad grin and clumsy walk.

You are a woman, phenomenally,

She promised,

And although I was only 11,

I felt I could respond, "Yes, that's me."

In Langston's lullabies,

I saw beauty in my frizzy curls and brown skin,

And even though I was from Brooklyn,

Imagined myself as his sweet Harlem girl.

I blossomed among Nikki Giovanni's lyrical lilacs,

Discovered my gardens in Alice Walker's prose,

And heard Lucille Clifton,

As she asked me to listen, child.

In their words, their gentle rhythms,

Repetitions, emphases, and pauses

I learned to write and love and like dust,

Rise.

—Maya Doig-Acuña, 2012 (used with permission)

I first heard this poem performed at a poetry slam. At the time, I was completely smitten by the poem and by the young woman who had always had a voice, but now began to sing and explain how the world made sense to her. Maya later became a student in my classes and has allowed me to use this poem in a presentation and again for this book. What struck me then, and now, are the words, "Yes, that's me," in response to poetry that spoke to a young brown skinned girl seeking a way to fit in school, to matter, to witness the world, and to be witnessed in return. This chapter explores how inclusive anti-racist teaching takes into account the *what*, *how*, and *who* of teaching. The work engages critical multicultural education and culturally relevant and sustaining pedagogy (Ladson-Billings, 2009; Paris, 2012). When a teacher places this work at the center of her teaching, students like Maya experience the multitude of possibilities of who they are and who they can be.

Multicultural education has too often been translated into a watered-down form of universalism, with some special events to celebrate "diversity" thrown in the mix. Today, at all levels of education, multicultural education is frequently touted in the one author of color taught in a course or represented in a "heroes and holidays" model. In this model, culture is reduced to celebrating "cultural" (read nonwhite) holidays, traditional dress, and "ethnic" food. While holidays, food, traditional dance, and costumes can be a part of a robust exploration of pluralism, they cannot be the only aspects present in multicultural education.

In the "heroes and holidays" approach to multicultural education, select historical figures are "celebrated" in very specific and narrow ways. We learn, for example, that Rosa Parks sat down on the bus because she was tired from a long day of work. We almost never learn of Claudette Colvin a 15-year-old African American student who refused to give up her seat to a white woman on a bus—9 months before Mrs. Parks' historic refusal. We don't learn of the connections between the two and how Parks was inspired in part to act because of Colvin. We rarely learn of Mrs. Parks' lifelong commitment to disrupting injustice, or of her formal training at the Highlander Folk School, which provided social justice leadership training, nonviolent desegregation strategies, and literacy programs (Theoharis, 2013). We get instead a safer version. We hear Dr. King's "I Have a Dream" speech and neglect to teach about the arc of his too short career. His critiques of capitalism, the Poor People's movement he was launching near the time of his death, and his adamant opposition to the Vietnam War are left out of most teachings.

The current presence of Black History Month as it is frequently undertaken (if at all) is a month of prescripted and oft repeated sterile sets of knowledge that highlight "exceptional" Black people. This does a huge disservice to all students. It does little to disrupt the white supremacist script that Carter G. Woodson sought to displace when calling for "Negro History Week," the precursor to Black History Month. There is, of course, a much more critical and engaged way to approach Black History Month. The problem is not Black History Month, it is in the narrow and tokenizing way it is often "celebrated."

As a nation we desperately need to understand that Black history *is* the history of the United States. That work is still needed. This was clearly shown when Trump spoke so vaguely about Frederick Douglass, in terms that made it unclear if he knew whether or not Douglass was alive or dead. Nowhere in Trump's convoluted comments was there the understanding of Douglass' towering role in history or of his pushing Abraham Lincoln to move away from his role of accepting slavery and supporting the Fugitive Slave Act to his eventual drafting of the Emancipation Proclamation. As journalist Charles Blow (2017) writes, "Frederick Douglass is a singular, towering figure of American history. The entire legacy of black intellectual

thought and civil rights activism flows in some way through Douglass..."
(p. A21). Teachers cannot rely on our leaders to help tell a more complete
story of the United States; it is up to us.

Which is why work must be done so that our curricula *engage* daily (and
not just during the month of February) with the multitude of racial identities and histories that make up the United States. I use Black History Month
as an example, but the list of stories, histories, perspectives, and *entire people
groups* that are completely ignored in the dominant curricula is exhaustive.
(To explore activities that engage the complexities of student identities see
Appendix F: "My Identity in School.")

I was once in an orientation workshop for cooperating teachers who
would be hosting student teachers from a local university. The facilitator
asked us to consider the aspects of our teaching that were crucial for student teachers to know and understand. We shared our thoughts with a partner. My partner emphatically told me how important it was for her student
teacher to be able to handle "the multicultural unit" she offered each fall.
At first, I honestly didn't understand what she meant. As she talked it was
clear she saw multiculturalism as a set aside unit that, once finished, the rest
of the "real" curricula could proceed apace.

I prefer the comprehensive definition of critical multicultural education provided by the renowned scholar and educator, Sonia Nieto (2002):

> Multicultural education is a process of comprehensive school reform for all
> students. It challenges and rejects racism and other forms of discrimination
> in schools and society and accepts and affirms the pluralism (ethnic, racial,
> linguistic, religious, economic, and gender among others) that students,
> their communities, and teachers reflect. (p. 29)

Nieto points out that multicultural education is a *process*—not a onetime
event or unit. It is rooted in a commitment to social justice and anti-racism
and is important basic education that provides a critical lens for all students. As the definition illustrates, multicultural education is much more
than a festival, a feast, or a "diverse" bulletin board. The work requires reflection and critical engagement with students. Consider the ways Isabelle
Klein (one of the anti-racist teachers introduced in the Chapter 2) frames
her work and the considerations she makes in preparing her class:

> When I decide what to teach, I have a pretty steady inventory of questions
> in my mind. Who am I including? Who am I leaving out? In what ways will
> students be able to identify with these texts? Who will feel represented in the
> literature? What kinds of discomfort might arise for students? Where do the
> texts intersect thematically with students' experiences?

What we teach matters and not just when there are students of color present in the classroom. Multicultural education is basic education for *all* students. One of the mistakes often made in conceptualizing multicultural education is that in order for students to relate to it, it must mean the same thing to all students. In many English and other literature classes there is a tendency to push towards universal themes. While finding common ground can be powerful, it must not be done to the point that the specificity of a text is lost. Quite often in this approach the subject of race and racial identity is marginalized or ignored completely. We can, of course, learn across difference and power. Students should be exposed to diverse texts, histories, and perspectives. However, we need to be able to address what is specific and unique about a particular text or viewpoint before norming it to a dominant or pluralistic standard. To illustrate, consider following examples of attempting to engage in inclusive anti-racist practice. Please note that the examples are of specific courses or specific texts within larger units. Merely teaching one book or bringing up the topic of race and racial identity in one play does not constitute multiculturalism. I use concrete specifics here to root these concepts to actual practice. These practices are nested into classrooms that center inclusive anti-racist pedagogy.

Representation Matters

I teach a course on the playwright August Wilson. Wilson's powerful body of work chronicled experiences of African Americans in every decade of the 20th century. His work is rich and lyrical. His characters, almost all of African descent, speak in vibrant language that place one in the time period of the play. Prior to moving to higher education, I had a chance to teach and direct Wilson's plays at the high school level. In these settings the power of what we teach and how we teach had become crystal clear to me. Though I have written elsewhere (Affolter, 2013) about teaching Wilson's plays, I want to highlight some of the joy that comes from working with material that speaks to Black students' history and the transformative power of that work. Early on in my work as a high school English and theatre teacher, I became frustrated with the Eurocentric nature of theatre and the plays that were frequently selected for production at multiracial high schools. One year, I decided to stage a production of August Wilson's, *The Piano Lesson*. Tyson, who had been known as a "troublemaker," was the lead, "Boy Willie," in the production. As an adult, Tyson wrote to me of the power of the play and of being recognized as something beyond a "troubled Black teen":

From the moment the school saw me on stage as "Boy Willie" I gained my
first positive identity at school. I was known for being good at something.
Being involved in *The Piano Lesson* was one of the reasons I petitioned our
school to add an African American history class. Being involved in the play
was one of the reasons I chose to move to Mississippi to further my education, as well as one of the reasons why I will stay here to help bring about
change to the impoverished conditions that African American people live in
down here. (Affolter, 2013, p. 110)

It was crucial to Tyson and to other students involved in the production to bear witness and honor a deeper understanding of their families'
histories. Many of the cast members had roots in Mississippi. Their families had moved to Illinois as part of the Northern Migration. Similarly, the
main characters in the *The Piano Lesson* had family members who had been
enslaved in Mississippi and now family members were grappling with that
history as they lived in the North. Family members came in to help dress
the set with family photographs, talk to students about how to use an old
fashioned hot comb, and tell stories about visiting Mississippi as children.
Beyond the historical and personal connections, it was also crucial for Tyson and (other cast members), to have others witness who he was and who
he could be in positive ways.

Offering opportunities for students to experience work like Wilson's
provides a space for voices that have never been silent but have often been
ignored. But it also is important for white students who may come to the
work with very different backgrounds and expectations.

Teaching material that specifically centers Black life and asking students to engage fully with the characters' identities and struggles offers a
chance for all students to expand their worldview. One can appreciate the
specificity of a text and see the connections to larger "universal themes"
without resorting to whitewashing the text or norming things to the dominant culture.

Not a Coloring Book

As a high school English teacher, I would frequently start my 10th grade
class with the text *House on Mango Street*, by Sandra Cisneros (1991). (Ref-
erenced in the introduction as well.) The book, a series of vibrant vignettes
about a Mexican American girl named Esperanza, is a perfect launching
pad for all students to explore their own identities. We talk and write about
gender, home, social class, race, and childhood. Students write their own
version of the book and the unit generally ends with an author's tea during

which students read a selection of their texts to invited audience members. All in all, it is an ideal book to introduce students to each other and to introduce the diversity of experiences and ideas that will make up our classroom.

I had done a version of this opening unit for a few years, but it wasn't until I met Maria and Alice that I realized that while I had opened up space for everyone to see themselves in the text, I had neglected to appreciate how specific experiences of Esperanza might speak to members of our class. I had fallen into the trap of using a text without engaging the specificity of the race and cultural richness in it. Instead, I used it as a coloring book for others and in doing so, erased some of its power.

This didn't occur to me until Maria and Alice came and asked if we had any copies of the book in Spanish. We had one in the book vault and I found another in a used bookstore and proudly presented the texts to the students the next day. From that moment onward (and long after we finished *House on Mango Street*) Maria and Alice were engaged participants in the class. They offered nuance about the stories that we missed in the English version, explained Spanish words and slang and giggled at the in-jokes of cultural traditions. They saw themselves in the text. It was a wake-up call for me. Despite my best intentions, by failing to meaningfully engage the culturally specific aspects of the text, I had fallen into the color-evasive, universal mode. The book benefited everyone, but by ignoring race or glossing over it to get to how it applied to all of us, I nearly lost an important opportunity for engagement and for students to say, "This is me."

White Communities Too

As discussed in the previous chapter, one of the mistakes surrounding concepts of multicultural education is that it is education for students of color and only needed if such students are physically present in the classroom. Working with teachers in rural Vermont, Erika Berger (discussed in previous chapter) and I sought to disrupt this myth by designing a unit around Julia Alvarez' (2009) young adult novel, *Return to Sender*. Our goal was to help foster an understanding of interdependence as teachers engaged meaningfully with race and racial identity. We chose this book because it is set in rural Vermont in the county and surrounding counties in which these teachers work. The novel uses the altering viewpoints of Tyler, a Vermont farm boy and Mari, a girl his age from Mexico. Tyler and Mari represent an interdependent tension that is very real in the rural Northeast. Mari and her family are migrant workers from Mexico hired by Tyler's father to help save the family farm. The novel explores the tensions of immigration, family customs, bilingual identity, cross-cultural and cross-racial friendships and racial isolation. The novel also brings to the fore issues of disability and cross-generational understanding. It does so in a way that allows both characters to speak and both characters to realize the connected nature of their lives.

However, it is not just a feel-good novel and deals honestly with personal and institutional racism and fear of the unknown. For example, in the opening scene of the novel Tyler, who hasn't been informed of the new hiring over the summer, runs to his parents yelling, "There are some Indians trespassing!" Tyler also goes through periods of being ashamed to have Mari as a friend and he judges his father for bringing Mari's family to the farm.

Mari's father and uncles spend much of their time living in fear of being deported, while searching for Mari's mother who has been kidnapped while trying to reenter the United States. Mari's younger sisters were born in the United States while Mari was born in Mexico. She is encouraged by her father to hide that part of her identity as much as possible.

We shared with teachers ways to situate discussions on race and racial identity not as a historicized past nor completely outside of students' and teachers' frames of reference. Instead of shying away from the prejudice voiced in the 12-year-old character of Tyler, we encouraged teachers to consider how they might confront that part of the novel. Could they imagine the same attitudes existing in their classrooms (or in themselves)? We encouraged them to read closely the sections written from Mari's point of view (Mari writes a series of postcards and letters throughout the novel). Perhaps they could ask students to write their own letter back to Mari? Finding ways to animate discussions with multiple viewpoints, even if those viewpoints start from literature and then come from students' lives is a crucial step in breaking down essentialized knowledge about some racialized "other" and moving to a more engaged and connected space.

These few examples demonstrate that content matters, and what we do with content matters. Acknowledging students' identity and building on their prior knowledge while pushing them to see beyond what they know are important pieces of a multicultural education. However, content alone is not enough to work towards embodying anti-racist and inclusive education. Pedagogy matters in concrete ways. One could teach many topics that could engage race, and not do so. Merely teaching a novel that touches on race or features characters of color does not constitute anti-racism in action unless the accompanying pedagogy builds and supports meaningful conversations and activities that allow authentic engagement with race to happen.

The beauty of engaging students at all levels and listening to what they have to say is that many of the answers to how to connect to all students are there, if we pay attention. Consider the poem that started this chapter. Maya clearly outlined how her 11-year-old self, craved material that acknowledged her existence and helped her "like herself." Offering a child, adolescent, or adult space to explore and open up possibilities of who they are, and who they can be is one of the crucial tasks for educators as we decide what and how to teach.

More Dream Keepers Needed

One successful approach that has influenced many educators is culturally relevant pedagogy. Pioneered by Gloria Ladson-Billings (1995), culturally relevant pedagogy (CRP) is built on three main concepts:

> (a) Students must experience academic success; (b) students must develop and maintain cultural competence; and (c) students must develop a critical consciousness through which they challenge the status quo of the current social order. (p. 60)

Anyone who has truly understood and applied these concepts to the whole of their teaching can attest to their transformative power. In her foundational work, *The Dreamkeepers: Successful Teachers of African American Children,* (2009), Ladson-Billings profiles teachers that embody culturally relevant practices. This is richly detailed qualitative research that brings us inside the classrooms and communities of exemplary teachers. There have been many who have built upon Ladson-Billings concept of CRP and as Ladson-Billings (2014) notes, "Scholarship is ever-changing." In her introduction piece to a special issue of the *Harvard Education Review,* "Culturally Relevant Pedagogy 2.0: a.k.a. the Remix," Ladson-Billings explains how scholars have used culturally relevant pedagogy

> as the place where "the beat" drops and then layer the multiple ways the notion of pedagogy shifts, changes, adapts, recycles, and recreates instructional spaces to ensure that consistently marginalized students are repositioned into a place of normativity—that is they become subjects in the instructional process, not mere objects. (p. 76)

Ladson-Billings' use of remix is particularly important here and gets at a potential tension between creation of theory and the adaptation of it within classrooms. While scholarship must morph and change, we also need to keep in mind what is happening in classrooms, what teachers are reading and how they are connecting theory to practice.

Beauboeuf-Lafontant (1999) looked at culturally relevant pedagogy among African American teachers and built on the third tenet of CRP, "developing a critical consciousness," where she asserts that the educators she studies are practicing "politically relevant teaching." She writes, "These educators recognized the existence of oppression in their students' lives and sought to use their personal, professional, and social power to encourage children to understand and undermine their subordination" (p. 702).

Building from CRP, Paris (2012) developed the theory of "culturally sustaining pedagogy (CSP)," a theory that has an explicit goal of

> supporting multilingualism and multiculturalism in practice and perspective for student and teachers. CSP seeks to perpetuate and foster—to *sustain*—the linguistic, literate, and cultural pluralism as part of the democratic project of schooling and as a needed response to demographic and social change. (p. 88)

Emdin (2016) builds on CRP by formulating a theory and practice of "reality pedagogy." His formulation consists of the "5 cs": cogenerative dialogues (dialogues that happen with educators and build on students' language and community traditions), coteaching (students are experts while the teacher is positioned as the novice), cosmopolitanism (human beings take responsibility for one another and individual difference is honored), context (students' home-culture is part of the classroom), and content (teacher builds content knowledge with students).

I highlight these three scholars because each adds important aspects to different remixes of culturally relevant pedagogy. However, as Ladson-Billings has pointed out, many teachers in classrooms have not mastered the basics (i.e., can't hear the beat, let alone dance to it) of CRP. Just as theory cannot be divorced from practice, it is important to be mindful of what is happening in classrooms. None of these remixes overreach or are disconnected from classrooms; however, many schools are still fumbling along with watered down versions of multiculturalism and incomplete notions of CRP. Culturally relevant pedagogy in the many forms and various theories that build off it (and that the theory itself has built upon) are important and thus worth examining more closely.

For those seeking empirical data of the power of culture relevance in disrupting patterns of inequity, Stanford's Center for Educational Policy Analysis released a study highlighting the efficacy of implementing culturally relevant pedagogy (Dee & Penner, 2016). This study "provides such evidence through examining the effects of a ninth-grade Ethnic Studies course piloted over several years in the San Francisco Unified School District (SFUSD)" (p. 2). To summarize, the study examined data from five cohorts of ninth grade students who had been enrolled in an Ethnic Studies course. (Ethnic Studies courses and programs are designed specifically to provide a counter narrative to whiteness through the study of literature, histories, and patterns of resistance and social movements of people of color.) Students were assigned to the course in eighth grade if they had been deemed at risk of dropping out of high school. The authors found that participation in such classes "increased student attendance (i.e., reduced unexcused absences) by 21 percentage points; cumulative ninth-grade GPA by 1.4 grade points, and credits earned by 23 credits" (Dee & Penner, 2016, p. 2).

The authors stress that such results happened when students were in highly supportive environments and *teachers maintained a high degree of fidelity to the foundations of culturally relevant pedagogy.* For this reason, I go back to the basics by examining and understanding each piece of Ladson-Billings original conception of CRP.

The first aspect of CRP is that "students must experience academic success." Read almost any mission statement from any school district and there is likely a phrase touting the goal of academic excellence and success for all. It is an idea dripping with good intentions that quickly fall away when presented with data that repeatedly shows that some of our students have a now well-known pattern of not succeeding in schools. The pattern is so predictable that we now have a popular phrase for it the, "achievement gap." This gap refers to the academic achievement between white students and students of color. Recall that this is language used to obscure the fact that we have systematically denied some students access to high quality education and academic success.

While elsewhere in this text I have pointed out the extremes of denying students of color the support and access needed for academic success, here I want to pause to examine the "nice" ways teachers, particularly white teachers, can sabotage student success.

Scenario 1: "Making Poor Choices"

A volunteer is working in a kindergarten classroom. She notices that frequently one student, Andre, an African American boy, does not participate in literacy center. Instead he wanders around the room, usually ending up near the Legos or cars and spends the literacy time quietly playing with those toys. After her third visit the volunteer asks, "Why isn't Andre joining the reading groups?" The teacher quickly explains that Andre is "making a poor choice," and that she hopes he will make "a better choice" in the future.

Andre is denied access to core literacy skills because no one is pushing him. The teachers' use of "poor choice" is telling here. As anyone who has worked with small children knows, playing is not at all a poor choice. (It is actually developmentally part of learning and growth.) Andre's play is not the problem. The point is that if literacy development is deemed important for advancement for the *rest* of the predominantly white class, why is Andre ignored in this way? Not all students need the same thing at the same time, but all students need to be provided rigorous and engaging opportunities for learning the skills required for their success. Benign neglect is one form of racism that white educators frequently employ for their Black and Brown students.

This was made especially clear to me when Jerry, once explained to me what he meant by "fake nice." In fourth grade he came home and announced, "Mom, it's not nice if you do something wrong and you don't get in trouble for it. That's like fake nice, not real nice." This was coming from a 9-year-old child who would, in time, have more than his share of both warranted and unwarranted punishment in school. As he explained, I realized he didn't want to be punished, he wanted to be respected as a student.

He and two of his friends, Peter and Clint (both white) had been goofing around in class one day and as a result, failed to complete the work assigned to them. Peter and Clint stayed inside with the teacher and finished their work, while Jerry was sent off to recess. He saw this as "fake nice." Rather than holding him accountable and helping him finish the work, the teacher held lower expectations for Jerry.

He later told me he much preferred the consistency and loving, but firm approach, of his third-grade teacher, "Mrs. Arnold." He said, "She was the same. If you didn't finish your work you had to finish it. Everyone did. If you were bad you got in trouble. But she treated you every day the same. Same if you were good. Same if you weren't. Same, same, same." I have tried for years to explain to preservice students how centering your practice in love and high expectations for all students really matters and my son did it in two phrases: don't' be "fake nice" and "same, same, same." Of course, we need to treat students as individuals and recognize the unique stories they bring with them to class. The same, same, same here that Jerry pointed out is the fact that Mrs. Arnold truly believed in each student and demanded academic excellence from each student in the class. Students in her class didn't walk away with a sense that some students were "bad" students and others were "good" students. They all had to work and she saw to it that each reached their academic capacity.

The reality is that adults need to intervene and insist on academic excellence for all students. In these stories and in countless other examples, we must ask who we allow to "make poor choices," and for whom "poor choices" are not an option. All students experiencing academic success means just that—all students are given the supports and teaching needed to succeed.

Scenario 2 "Taking Care of a Friend"

"Adrian" a former student, tells me about her early experiences in being denied reading instruction. In second grade Adrian, who is Black, was constantly called upon to comfort one of her white friends, "Sarah" in class. Apparently, Sarah was having trouble adjusting to school and would quickly become overwhelmed and cry. When this happened, Adrian was asked repeatedly to go out in the hall with her crying friend and comfort her. After several episodes of this, Adrian grew bored and came back into the classroom to join a reading group. The teacher asked Adrian, "What are you doing here? Where is Sarah?" When Adrian explained that Sarah was still in the hall, she was sent back to join Sarah and told, "Don't come back without her being ready to join the group."

In this scenario the "nice white teacher" plays into a number of racialized and gendered stereotypes. As discussed in Chapter 1, white women are often constructed as racially pure, helpless, and in need of protection and help. One of the most insidious tropes in relationship to Black women is the "Mammy." The "Mammy" stereotype presents Black women as put on this earth to comfort, serve, and protect white families. In the above scenario, though only 9, Adrian is forced into the role of caretaking and protecting her white peer. While there is nothing wrong with supporting peers in their learning, Adrian is denied opportunities to learn because she is forced to comfort her friend Sarah. Apparently, alleviating Sarah's anxiety or general displeasure in school is more important than Adrian gaining access to crucial literacy skills. Insisting that a student, particularly a student of color, become a permanent "teacher's helper" is "fake nice." Again, demanding excellence from *all* students requires that all teachers examine their own biases and ways they might not engage *all* students. Further, it demands that teachers push themselves to ensure that all students have access to high quality instruction and to the learning that goes on in the classroom.

Which brings us to the next piece of culturally relevant pedagogy: *developing and maintaining cultural competence.* Paris (2012) and Paris and Alim

(2017) have especially built on this aspect of CRP in introducing the concept of culturally sustaining pedagogy, which seeks to "perpetuate and foster—to sustain—linguistic, literate, and cultural pluralism as a part of the democratic project of schooling and as a needed response to demographic and social change" (2014, p. 88). Students' language, culture, and home matter.

Consider Femi's remarks to the power of sustaining and celebrating linguistic pluralism. Femi is another cast member from my first production of *The Piano Lesson*. Here she talks about how being in the play, followed by a production of *The Wiz* (a Black version of the *The Wizard of Oz*) allowed her to appreciate her own voice, quite literally. She writes,

> It wasn't until *The Wiz* that I realized my Blackness had a unique impact on the role I was playing. I could speak using my more relaxed dialect, and it helped the part. I could sing the way I was taught in the Black church, and it made the song sound better. And I can't quite remember the sequence of what show I was in after that, but I know that I was resolved to be all of who I was in everything I did from then on. I remember that a teacher once commented that she had heard me talking in the hallway to my friends, and it sounded different than when I talked to her in my class. I was embarrassed by that. Not the case after being in these shows. People actually got to see the complete Femi, know that I was multi-faceted, and accept it. Or not... (Affolter, 2013)

Instead of seeing students as receptacles for only the knowledge that the teacher and curricula dictates, the culturally relevant (and anti-racist) teacher builds on the knowledge, prior experiences, language traditions, family, neighborhood, and community cultural histories.

I once had my 10th graders conduct interviews with community elders. They could choose anyone over 50 (elder being a loose term here) from their family, community, or church and discuss two questions: "What is home?" and "What made a good community?" Students brought in interviews from family and community: grandparents, aunts, uncles, barbers, ministers, and local restaurant owners. Everyone interviewed was then invited to a reception, during which the students read from their pieces. All the interviews were assembled into a book that students were able to take home with them.

I loved this project. Community members showed up and applauded the students and took the time to meet one another. Over punch and cookies, I witnessed a Hmong father talking with another student's white uncle about gardens while a Hmong student translated. I saw students put on their best selves as they introduced me to pastors and parents. It was a really great day.

But what I loved more was the day *after* the formal presentation. One of the students had interviewed a Black barber who was somewhat famous in Madison, Wisconsin. I saw many of my Black male students bonding and laughing about the lessons they had learned from sitting in this elder's chair. They laughed about the fades their mothers insisted they get before school pictures (and compared notes on a crooked lineup caught forever in a photo). They nodded in agreement about how grown up they felt when they first sat in that chair.

Soon, as class started, I invited some of the students to share about the unique culture of Black barbershops. What followed was a rich discussion about all sorts of cultural traditions in Black communities, in Hmong families, and in white working-class homes. Students shared the knowledge of their communities with pride and we all learned a great deal from one another. All of this was done while furthering academic skills. This was not an aside that had nothing to do with content or standards. Such work can only happen if we value students' lived experiences, their cultural capital, and communities. Ms. Jameson (a teacher introduced earlier) sees challenging the erasure of students' identity and cultural representations as central to her work:

> I feel like what different groups have in common with one another, one of the things is the struggle of invisibility. A lot of the struggles they are facing are not visible to other people who are not facing the same struggle. That invisibility, if I feel invisible, I can never be deeply known, my gifts can never be deeply part of the making of the world. I guess one of the big changes I would like to see is that meta-understanding to begin to grow among people. Because if I know that somebody who is a stranger to me, who is different from me, has gifts for me to understand and learn from, then I am going to have a very different approach than if I just assume we are on the same plane and we both just sort of understand the same things and have the same general perspective, because we are both human beings. I would like to see more of that meta-awareness, that there are differences and we need to try to learn from each other.

The concept of truly seeing another person and learning from her is interwoven into Ms. Jameson's definition of social justice and anti-racist work. In the following comments we again see firm examples of culturally relevant pedagogy and anti-racist teaching:

> I think that social justice is a way of interacting between people in which people are very much trying to see the other person for who they are and find a way to appreciate them for who they are, without trying to make them like me. Because I think trying to make somebody else like me is the root of violence.

Earlier I introduced the concept of the cultural deficit model. In this model students of color and their families are seen as lacking in multiple ways. Many educators who went through university-based teacher training programs will be familiar with the concept of cultural capital. In brief, sociologist Pierre Bourdieu (1986) critiqued the ways school replicated inequity by rewarding middle and upper-class traditions, customs, ways of speaking, and basic dispositions (habitus). In rewarding these traits, hierarchical class structure was replicated across generations. Bourdieu largely neglected race, but the basic concept about rewarding only certain types of cultural capital remained. Schools cater to white middle and upper-class students' speech, habits, and basic dispositions. Classrooms most match up with the cultural backgrounds that these students bring to school and students are rewarded for this match. For teachers, the message was, and often still is, that we need to help the students whose backgrounds don't match with the dominant group "fit." The talents, skills, and cultural backgrounds students from nondominant groups bring with them to the classroom are seen as deficient. Thus, the kind thing to do is to help these "disadvantaged" students catch up and be more like the dominant group.

A better alternative to the cultural capital theory is what critical race scholars have termed "community cultural wealth" (Yosso, 2005). In this model, aspects of communities of color that are typically dismissed, ignored, or belittled are instead honored. Community cultural wealth takes many forms including aspirational, navigational, social, linguistic, familial, and resistant capital. Each of these aspects of community cultural wealth builds on one another and none have a single or static definition. They connect because they force a consideration of what is considered "the norm" and how the norm is read and rewarded in classrooms. For example,

> *Familial capital*...engages a commitment to community well-being and expands the concept of family to include a broader understanding of kinship....familial capital is nurtured by our "extended family," which may include immediate family (living or long passed on) as well as aunts, uncles, grandparents, and friends who we might consider part of our *familia*. (Yosso, 2015, p. 79)

Imagine if familial capital was utilized as a strength that students bring to the classroom rather than a difference to be overcome? What rich stories, insights, and wisdom could students and teachers learn from one another?

Consider Ms. Kline's unit regarding justice and injustice as an example of how one might utilize another aspect of community cultural wealth, "navigational capital":

One really great teaching experience has been designing a writing project called perspective poems. After reading, *A Gathering of Old Men*, by Ernest Gaines (a novel told through multiple narrators that follows the aftermath of the murder of a Cajun farmer in Louisiana in the 1970s) and viewing Anna Deavere Smith's *Twilight* (a series of monologues written from actual interviews with people from Los Angeles following the acquittal of the police officers who beat Rodney King [For younger readers, King, a Black man, was severely beaten by LA police officers in 1991. The beating was caught on videotape—in a time before cell phone cameras—and the footage was shared around the world. When the officers were acquitted of the crimes several days of rioting—or uprising depending on who is telling the story—broke out in Los Angeles.]), I ask students to identity a moment of conflict or injustice in their own lives. Students then write about the event from three different points of view (including their own).

It's an interesting lesson, because there are inevitably white students who say, "I've never experienced injustice." This is a great opportunity for some powerful discussions.

Ms. Kline continued to explain how Black, Hmong, and Latino students share about the ways they experienced injustice and were presumed guilty, dangerous, not "normal" or illegal in simple daily interactions. Examples included being followed in stores; stopped for hall passes; questioned about where they are "from;" witnessing parents being denied a variety of services because the waiter, clerk, or DMV agent couldn't "understand" what they were saying. One student discussed how the paperwork she brought to school to prove residency was rejected by an attendance secretary and told, "there is no way you live there." Though Ms. Kline didn't name it as such, this activity offers an opportunity for students of color to celebrate their navigational capital. It is a chance for white students to learn about the privileges they take for granted and for students of color to demonstrate their own perseverance in such situations. In the activity is highlighting "the ability to maneuver through institutions not created with Communities of Color in mind" (Yosso, 2005, p. 80).

This example also ties into the final aspect of culturally relevant pedagogy (one that is frequently overlooked), "Students must develop a critical consciousness through which they challenge the status quo of the current social order" (Ladson-Billings, 1995, p. 60). Once again, Sage, offers insight on the danger of lacking a critical consciousness. Instead of providing tools to critique and demand change, students are frequently left without the crucial skills or information they need to develop a critical consciousness.

This in part due to the way whiteness thrives, reproduces, and obscures the need to question and thus allows and encourages incomplete education.

In the majority of the preceding examples I have described teachers who employ culturally relevant pedagogy in multiracial classrooms.

But whiteness also depends on poor whites buying into and promoting white supremacy. This is complicated because while poor whites can be used to leverage the white supremacist agenda and sustain whiteness, they are also denied access to power and privileges granted to middle class or wealthy whites. In the following example I present a course I co-created that attempted to deliberately disrupt the racism present in poor white rural America while supporting critical consciousness to the students in the class.

The Unfinished Business of the Poor People's Campaign

In the Fall of 2013, I co-designed and co-taught with Deirdre Kelly, a teacher at the Addison County Parent Child Center (PCC) a course entitled, "Exploring the Unfinished Business of the Poor People's Campaign." The course was created for students at the PCC who were enrolled in the high school diploma completion program.

Briefly, the Addison Country Parent Child Center, located in Middlebury, Vermont provides support and education to young families. One important aspect of the center is the alternative education program that allows pregnant and parenting young adults to earn high school credit through academic courses, on the job training, therapeutic groups, and hands-on parenting skill building. Participants in the alternative education program are able to earn their high school diploma while being provided specific support unique to the needs and goals of young parents.

Students enrolled in our course participated in an examination of literature and history surrounding low income people's struggles for civil rights. A main goal of the course was to uncover, highlight, and celebrate the ways that grassroots movements led by the poor have made a difference.

Through a variety of critical reading, writing, and thinking exercises the teachers sought to support the participants at PCC in realizing the expertise they have in battling economic injustice. Participants engaged in journaling, storytelling, collecting local oral histories, and other forms of community outreach as they moved to their own understanding of themselves as agents of social/economic change. A few guiding questions for the course included: How do we redefine what counts as knowledge? How do we support young people from marginalized communities to enable them to view their knowledge and insight as important while appreciating the context of their struggle within a historical landscape of poor people fighting for economic justice? What ways do we go about disrupting the racism that the students in our classes expressed while at the same time empowering their voices?

All the course participants were white women living at or below the poverty line; most already had one child. All were familiar with public assistance in some way and most have been homeless or in situations where housing and/or food were insecure. They were very familiar with concepts of inequity as it applied to their daily reality.

The challenges we faced as instructors became clear on the first day. We explained the origins of the *Poor People's Campaign.* King and other leaders of the Southern Christian Leadership conference had organized the Poor People's Campaign that brought people from across the country to Washington, DC to present Congress with a list of demands for economic justice and then set up a 3,000-person tent city to draw attention to the living conditions of the poor. In summary, the campaign sought to highlight the overarching demand that all people should have what they need to survive. Though King did not live to see the protest itself (he was assassinated a month before the march took place) the ideals of the Poor People's Campaign were present in all of his work. For example, in his 1964 Nobel Prize acceptance speech, King said,

> I have the audacity to believe that peoples everywhere can have three meals
> a day for their bodies, education and culture for their minds, and dignity,
> equality, and freedom for their spirits. (King, 1964a, para. 7)

On the first day of class we pulled quotes from his March 31, 1968 sermon "Remaining Awake Through a Great Revolution," that highlighted the persistence of racism and how poverty and war exacerbated these issues. In the speech King correctly pointed out that, "There is nothing new about poverty. What is new is that we now have the techniques and the resources to get rid of poverty. The real question is whether we have the will" (King, 1968, n.p.). Suffice it to say that both teachers were convinced and inspired by King's work and felt certain this would be a perfect entry to discussing race and class inequality. I was not prepared for students' lack of racial and historical knowledge.

And at first, I was shocked and somewhat judgmental of these students. I showed a variety of clips of Dr. King speaking. After the clips one student said "that the 'I Have a Dream' guy, right?" I told her that yes that was one of his most famous speeches. She then followed up with "He got shot right? Is he dead?" It would be easy to dismiss this student and her peers as some sort of anomaly. It is frightening how easy it is to fall into predictable patterns of classism and make assumptions about which types of white people are racially aware. The truth is, though, the lack of racial literacy across this country and particularly in white enclaves is hardly rare. Instead of judging this student it was important to both teachers that we honor where students were from and move from there.

In another session before class started a student, "Stephanie," a powerful leader in the class, began talking about how much she loved her friend's "mulatto baby." A discussion ensued and students began listing the different terms they used to describe biracial or multiracial people they knew. Stephanie insisted loudly that "mulatto" was the correct term to refer to people of Black and white parentage. As teachers we did not foresee this discussion, but it was a moment that needed to be addressed directly. We explained that the term is considered derogatory in the United States and talked a bit about how race was defined and the concept of the one-drop rule. We told students of the word's roots to Spanish and Portuguese words meaning "of the mule." Stephanie was defensive saying, "That was what I was taught was okay to say." She remained quiet the rest of the class. In future classes though she bounced back to her stellar leadership and later made a reference to "what she used to say" when talking about multiracial identity.

Despite some of these unplanned twists, we were deeply committed to concept building from what students knew and reinforcing that they had powerful lived experiences to bring to a course on economic injustice. Early in the class we asked students to define various socioeconomic categories. We placed chart paper around the room with the words poor, rich, and middle class on the top of each. Students were to walk around the room and write their associations with each word. At first no one wrote much and then there was a lot of activity around the rich and middle-class boards. I noticed Stephanie was growing increasingly agitated as the activity went on. She scribbled in large letters, "I don't like being poor." When we reconvened to read the charts, there were some heartbreaking basic needs included on the middle-class list. Running water, heat, and being able to buy your own food were all listed as middle-class luxuries. As we continued to debrief we feared that our activity had backfired. Instead of helping students see their own resilience we had instead created lists in which wholly negative attributes were clustered around the poor. Fed up with the litany of lacking that was on the poor list Stephanie rocketed from her chair, grabbed a sticky note, wrote in huge letters, "STRONG" and slapped it on the top of the poor list. We had our launching point to explore movements and actions of solidarity of poor people in U.S. history. We had our chance for students to look around the room and begin to say, "This is me."

As the class moved on we delved more into King's work, studied Mother Courage, examined current local public policies, conducted interviews with community members, and visited Middlebury College to give a presentation entitled "What I Wish My Teachers Knew," to prospective teachers.

About half way through the class, we studied Cesar Chavez and his work with the United Farm Workers. The students were riveted by this story and made powerful connections to their own community. They were impressed by the successful boycotts and protests led by the UFW and Chavez. Middlebury is located in rural Vermont and surrounded by farm communities. Many dairy farms in the area employ migrant workers. We invited members of Migrant Justice, an organization dedicated to farmworkers' rights, to speak to our class. The group has been working throughout Vermont to ensure that farmworkers are treated with dignity and respect and are provided adequate housing, working conditions, transportation, and healthcare access.

Jake, a white volunteer from Migrant Justice translated for Gabriel, a Latino farmworker from Mexico. Gabriel shared that when he first came to Vermont his housing consisted of a one-bedroom house shared by 10 men. The men slept in shifts due to lack of space. He explained how isolating it was to work on rural farms without transportation or access to familiar food. He talked about how he was unprepared for the harsh winters. The women listened intently, some asking questions others interjecting, "That is bullshit," when they heard about some hardship facing the workers. They also nodded in agreement at some points—how hard it is to sleep in an unheated home and the unreasonable cost of food.

After Gabriel and Jake left, we talked to the class about what they had learned. One of the students, Ashley, had grown up on a dairy farm and her family had employed Latino farm workers. She shared,

> I have to admit I was really nervous about today. I mean on the farm it always seemed that those guys were always just staring at me. I was always kind of scared. Today as the guy was talking I kept thinking about how much we had in common. But I was also thinking about how it must really suck to be in a place that you don't even have a way to get to town or no one speaks your language.

There were more small moments like this throughout the class. All of the students' final projects had something to do with economic justice in the community, including letters to the editor discussing the difficulty of teen mothers finding work and meetings with local politicians to discuss housing shortages. I share these examples because inclusive anti-racist work helps build the capacity of all students. In the case of PCC, we helped chip away a bit at whiteness while supporting a marginalized community of poor white teen mothers to see their own strengths.

We supported the PCC students as they moved to a commitment to collective, not just individual "empowerment," a final key to culturally relevant pedagogy. This means, among other things, we must help students interrogate the basic myth of the American Dream. To reiterate, this myth is rooted in individual achievement and exists detached from a variety of institutional realities such as subpar education for poor white children and many children of color from all economic backgrounds. The myth obscures the truth lurking behind the school-to-prison pipeline or the racial achievement "gap." Instead of perpetuating this myth, inclusive anti-racist teachers must shift the narrative such that students see the inequity that is built into the system. A key goal of inclusive anti-racist work is to replace the myth of meritocracy with an understanding that we aren't diminished by others' success.

6

Dangerous Nice White Lady

The Need for Critical Community

Brother Child

Brother child broke down two days ago, he broke down two days ago
    and don't think he's gonna get up.
See he never got that opportunity to grow up, never got that chance
    to grow up and
You can't grow in a box
And they kept shoving him into a box and
You can't grow in a ten by ten and they kept shoving him into a ten by
    ten and
You can't grow in the backseats of cop cars or cells with iron bars
and they kept putting him into a box.

Brother child broke down two days ago, he broke down two days and
    don't think he's gonna get up
And he never got that chance, he never got that chance to grow up,
And he doesn't know what to tell his mother or his sister or his two-
    year old daughter
And he's only 18.

Through the Fog, pages 109–125
Copyright © 2019 by Information Age Publishing
All rights of reproduction in any form reserved.

Brother child broke down two days ago, he broke down two days ago
You can pinpoint the moment, you can pinpoint the moment,
He's in the classroom and the teacher says to him, well, she said to
     him, she didn't say
"put down the gun,"
She didn't say, "Put down the hate."
She didn't say, "Put down the knife."
She told him, "Put down the pen: you're on my time and you've failed
     my test again.
PUT DOWN THE PEN."

He broke down two days ago, my brother broke down two days ago.
Brother child broke down two days ago and I'm scared,
I'm terrified because my brother
won't get up.

—Ali Muldrow, 2005 (unpublished, used with permission)

Ali Muldrow is an artist poet, activist, teacher, mentor, and community leader. She wrote "Brother Child" towards the end of her high school career. She spent 12 years in the public education system, years in which she was told by teachers the limits of who she could be and what she could do. Ali was frequently discouraged from taking challenging courses and was coached in multiple ways to be quieter, more compliant, and to consider her "limitations." Luckily for all of us, Ali ignored the "kind" advice or "well-meaning teachers" and continues to push boundaries. I had the honor of teaching Ali and working with her to develop a Spoken Word program at our high school. Had she heeded the advice of the teachers that continually underestimated her and suggested she scale back her aspirations, had she "put down her pen" the community would have lost an invaluable voice. This chapter specifically examines the danger of "nice white teachers" and how inclusive anti-racist teachers must work in community to avoid the pitfalls that lead to counseling students of color to accept and expect less from their education.

Kill Whitey Stuff?

It was one of those powerful teacher moments where, briefly, you can feel like you made a difference. We (two other teachers and myself) had pulled off our school's first poetry slam. Our students, many of whom were students of color and had never been involved in any school activity before, had stood in front of their classmates and passionately performed words of pride, words of pain, words that screamed, "This is me!" Their classmates responded with whistles of praise, shouts of recognition, giggles of delight. Our students spoke of history, family, race, anger, and love. After the performance, the artists (our students) dined on pizza while recounting their favorite moments, quoting each other's poems and savoring the feeling of being heard.

I swept out of the post-poetry pizza party and headed to my fifth hour class. As I approached my hallway a teacher called to me, "Hey, Tara, nice job with the poetry slam; I hear it was a bunch of kill whitey stuff." I stood stunned, wondering what would cause such a reaction. The bell rang and I wandered into my classroom.

How could anyone sit in that auditorium, feel that energy, hear those words, and come away with such a feeling? How could anyone who truly came to listen walk away with such a message of hate? As had become my coping strategy with such jarring breaks between my reality and the reality of many of my colleagues, I simply ignored the comment and hurried in to my classroom, to the safety of the community of my students. Together my students and I could challenge, discuss, listen to each other, and learn. Somehow, over the years, I had lost the opportunity to do this with most of my colleagues.

Turning Point

As I neared the end of my public-school teaching career, I had reached a point of crisis. This was not the usual, "Teacher burnout, I'm tired of the kids and grading crisis." I still felt the daily surge of joy while teaching classes and connecting with my students.

My crisis, rather, involved the adults around me. In the past year I had become one of the staff leaders for in-services around race and inequity. After only 8 months in that role, I approached each session ready for a fight. I no longer expected any conversations about racism in my school to be anything but a painful exercise in denial. My last session with the staff had started with a colleague calling out, "Tera, [at least get my name right!] if this is just another discussion of racism, why don't you just tell us why it is important so we can move on?" In short, battling racism had become "my issue."

Feeling the dread of another failed discussion approaching, I felt trapped and alone. Not having the strength for the peppy facilitator role needed, I took the coward's way out and typed up some possible discussion prompts for my "small group" of 70 staff. I sulked down to the cafeteria feeling defeated and ineffective. "I have some ideas you might want to discuss."

I held up the stack of papers, dropped them on the table in front of me and waited for the usual cliques to form.

I began scanning the room for a supportive cluster I might invade. I caught the eye of a soft-spoken woman who had always seemed very "present" in previous discussions. She smiled and I joined her table. Without much ado, I let loose about how angry I was at the staff. How they had spent an entire academic year clinging to deficit model thinking and acting wounded about having their white privilege pointed out to them. I don't know how long I talked, but I know she heard me. She paused and told me this story. (She credits the story to the great Buddhist monk, Milarepa [c. 1052–c. 1135 CE] and later sent me this transcribed version of the story.):

> When a monk approached his master to seek help in his path to enlightenment, he was troubled by the presence of continued anger in his heart. He felt that the anger was blocking his further growth and development. No matter how much he fasted and meditated, he felt he was not growing toward Buddha nature. The master told him he must seek deep within his heart for the source of his anger. The monk decided that he must go and seek the monster of his anger and slay him.
>
> The monk went off into a cave far away in the mountain where he meditated, prayed, and fasted for many days. Finally, the demon of his anger appeared as a great, many-headed monster. He fought the beast for many hours until he felt too exhausted to continue. But finally, with a great WOOSH of his sword, he cut the heads off of the beast, whereupon he fell, exhausted onto the floor. But lo and behold, the great beast rose back to its feet, much bigger than before, with a giant head and the most terrible expression the man had ever seen. The great monk felt powerless to fight and felt himself succumb to the monster as it opened its giant jaws to swallow him. Then, just as he believed he was about to take his last breath, he looked into the eyes of the beast and saw that it was none other than a reflection of himself. It was his own fear he was looking upon at the moment of his death. He was overcome with an overwhelming compassion for the creature, and as he stared into its eyes, it became transformed into a small child, his own memory of himself, whom he held in his arms with tears of great joy.

I can honestly report in that moment, bathed in the harsh fluorescent lights of the cafeteria, was an epiphany for me. For most of that year I had allowed others to use me as a dumping ground for their own fear disguised as anger. The result was that I had given up on the adults around me. I had built my own wall of anger and fear; anger that no one would listen; fear of the work I would really have to do if they did; fear that I wouldn't know where to begin if they listened. This woman, Ms. Jameson, later agreed to be part of my study on anti-racist teachers, but before that, she reminded me to look within myself and address those fears and my own limits. What fear was I not admitting? What was I avoiding? What was standing in the way of my work? What allies had I failed to see because of my own fear, anger, and ego? How was I making this about my own fatigue when people of color battle these issues every day? How was I, despite my deepest convictions, avoiding the work of anti-racism because I had made it about me and was simply scared of failing?

Throughout this book I have worked against the notion of the white hero. By now I hope to have established the fact that there is no stopping point, no t-shirt at the end of the race, no medal that declares one a champion crossing the finish line of racial justice. However, the isolation and alienation I often feel when working with white colleagues combined with accolades and celebrations I collect as a "nice white lady" that talks about race, can make for a dangerous cocktail. I can shut down and feel that I have "done enough" or demonize other white people thereby assuaging my own guilt or feelings of despair. Falling into the trap of the white hero "rescuing" students of color from *those racist* people is dangerous for a number of reasons.

I Can Do Alright in Here

Throughout my public-school teaching career, I made a point of standing outside my classroom door to greet students as they entered. It was a way for me to check in with each student individually. Sometimes I had students re-enter if they didn't seem ready for class or if they ignored my greeting. This time allowed me to signify that our classroom community started the moment they stepped inside the room. I could not control what had happened elsewhere that day, but I could insist on a supportive community during our 50 minutes together. It also gave me a chance to transition from one class community to the next. I looked forward to seeing the majority of my students each day. I had students who I knew challenged me more than others. And, to be honest, I had students who were secretly my favorites.

Kemple was one of my favorite 10th graders. (I know we aren't supposed to have favorites, but any teacher will tell you that there are students that especially steal pieces of their hearts.) When he was my student he was at that awkward 15-year-old boy/man phase. His body was going through a growth spurt, with his feet seeming to lead the way. He did not yet have much facial hair and wore his hair in braids sometimes adorned with white beads. Each day he wore a different crisp and oversized NBA jersey, baggy jeans, and some pristine (and huge) basketball shoes. It became a joke between us as he greeted me before class. He would hold up his foot, I would inspect and ask what size his feet had grown to overnight. He would flash a huge grin, shake his head, "Dang Ms. A." and move into class.

One day our ritual was significantly disrupted. Kemple rushed down the hall, a look of distress on his face and ran into the classroom. I turned to follow him and to find out what was wrong. Just as he took his seat an older white male teacher stormed towards Kemple's desk. Kemple shot to his feet. Though in the midst of his growth spurt the difference between this 15-year-old and a full-grown man was striking. Kemple may have been the same height, but this teacher dwarfed his thin frame.

I stepped between the two as the teacher began to yell at Kemple and at me. "Is this your student?" I told him it was. "Well, you better tell him he needs to watch himself." I thought it was an odd thing for an adult to say to a student. The teacher continued, "What's his name? What's his name?"

At that point Kemple was getting more agitated. "Get him out of here Ms. A." I asked the teacher to step into the hall. He came reluctantly but not without shouting again, "You better watch yourself, young man." I talked to the teacher and discovered that Kemple and another student had been splashing water at each other in the bathroom and were not aware that the teacher was approaching the sink. The teacher got wet and lost his cool. I am not sure what he said to the boys in the bathroom: Kemple never said more to me than, "That dude is crazy," but it was enough to unsettle Kemple, whose usual approach to the world was a grin and a shrug.

After I sent the teacher away (promising him I would handle it), I re-entered the classroom. Kemple was still standing. He punched the air, "Man, Ms. A. in here I can do alright, but I walk out there, and there's that."

I knew what he meant. I knew that Black males are not allowed to be children long before they are adults. I knew that while splashing water on one another might not be the most mature activity—it is not criminal. It is not behavior that deserves physical intimidation and threats. I knew that I was glad that Kemple had my classroom to come to and that I could shut my door and teach.

But what I didn't do is a product nice white talk. I didn't follow up with my colleague. Instead, I was content protecting Kemple from the mean white man. I was the hero in the moment and that was enough. The dream of my classroom being an oasis lulled me into a sense that was all I needed to do. I could distance myself from *those other* teachers and ignore the systemic and individual racism present around me because in *my* classroom students felt safe.

At the start of this book I discussed the notion of nice white talk (McIntyre, 1997). This is talk that ultimately protects whites from being challenged about racist beliefs and prevents real change for whites attempting to engage in anti-racist practice. Leonardo (2002) takes this a step further and points out the danger in avoiding discomfort:

> A pedagogy of politeness only goes so far before it degrades into the paradox of liberal feel-good solidarity absent of dissent, without which any worthwhile pedagogy becomes a democracy of empty forms. White comfort zones are notorious for tolerating only small, incremental doses of racial confrontation. (Leonardo, 2002, p. 33)

Leonardo is referencing class discussions and other moments of possible tension regarding authentically engaging with race and naming racism. But his words resonate to the situation with Kemple and many others. Too often I chose the path of closing my door and teaching rather than engaging in the larger work of systemic change. This is not to create an either/or dichotomy. My students will be at the forefront of my work for the remainder of my career. But the myth that I am enough, that I know enough, and that my individual resistance to racism is enough is ludicrous. Such a belief is fed and sustained by messages of unique white exceptionalism. Messages I must actively resist. I must do the work. I must examine my own teaching practices and yes, it is fine to stand in solidarity with people of color. But when I retreat, when I fail to engage the larger issues, or fail to confront other whites, I inch towards the very empty forms of pedagogy that Leonardo warns against.

Wise (2005) writes, "Resistance (of racism) takes work, it takes practice and it helps to have as much support as possible" (p. 85). To challenge school policies such as racial tracking systems; to confront fellow teachers when one witnesses a racist act; to interrogate one's own teaching practices and curriculum; to stand up to racism even at great personal risk, it helps to have a wider circle of support. I want to be cautious here even as I advocate for community. One cannot sit by and wait for consensus in the face of racist acts.

When I witnessed racist acts in the hallways of a school, I spoke out about them. I talked to the teacher or in some cases talked to the teacher's supervisors about what I witnessed. (Unfortunately, these events, often involving overt racist acts such as physically intimidating Black students happened relatively frequently. I have been able to practice my commitment to disrupting these issues with unsettling regularity.) I have not always handled these situations perfectly, nor has my reception at school following such incidents been particularly warm, nor have my actions resulted in lasting change at the various schools I have worked. Since moving to academia the need to challenge whiteness has not diminished. However, I remain convinced that remaining silent is unacceptable. My silence colludes with the racist act and is simply part of the dominant white culture that tolerates and encourages the privileging of whiteness over people of color.

My struggles with this work are not a result of bravery or superiority. For me, I act out of fear of what happens as we continue down this path, replicating year after year the same racist systems. I fear for my son and fear for his future children. I fear for my students and their families. I fear for my world and myself. But I also act from a place of hope.

Small Stones and Birthday Songs

During my sabbatical year, when much of this book was written, I volunteered at a bilingual (Spanish and English) elementary school located just down the street from our apartment in Cambridge, Massachusetts. Though I don't speak Spanish, I was invited to work with literacy groups (in English) in a kindergarten class. Each week I was infused with hope. I watched a multiracial, multiethnic, multilingual group of 5-year-olds learn from each other, teach each other, love each other, and grow.

The teachers in the class, both women of color hailing from Mexico and Chile, built a magical community. Their classroom was full of energy and the celebration of what made each person in the room unique. Even I, as a twice a week volunteer, was welcomed and appreciated for what I could bring to the group (my English teacher skills turned out to be useful after all.)

I witnessed students singing Happy Birthday in Spanish and English to one of their classmates from India and then excitedly explaining to me that the birthday boy celebrated on two different days in his culture. One student yelled to me, "WE GET TO SING TWICE!" I saw three African American boys figure out how to all hold hands so they could dance in a circle and then saw them stand still and look into each other's eyes smiling long after the music stopped. A white girl whose first language was English pulled me aside and tells me, "I've got some good news. The good news is I like to read." Then she looked at me as if she was about to break some bad news and said, "I like to read in Spanish better, but English is pretty good too." An African American boy pressed a small stone he found on the playground into my hand as a way of thanking me for helping him read one day. A white boy praised his Latinx friend during sharing time for her "really cool math solution." When a classmate returned from 3 months in Cambodia, where her family lived, her friends hustled to make sure she had a place in the class and was included in all of the groups. I witnessed students of all races slipping in and out of Spanish and English and patiently taking the time to help me learn Spanish (once cheering for me when I got the morning greeting right). I see all of this as hope. This class is a space where difference is truly honored and multiple voices are heard in a variety of ways. This is the type of inclusive anti-racist community that demonstrates the power of love in action in the classroom.

There Are Only Green Crayons, But We Can Work With This

Such hope helps with the sting of isolation and the web of resistance encountered by anti-racist educators. However, it would be helpful and more productive if, in addition to the individual stances against racism, inclusive anti-racist educators could find greater community and support for our work.

A related danger in embodying the white hero syndrome is an arrogance in thinking one is the *only* one doing the work. Such a stance results in the loss of crucial opportunities to learn from others. As such, the chance to have one's privilege (and perhaps martyrdom?) checked is eliminated. Further, sustaining the work both on a personal and institutional level is difficult, if not impossible to do alone.

Consider this example from Ms. Jameson who received a wake-up call in an early teaching experience:

> I had a chance to teach at Malcolm X Academy. When I got there, we got our box of supplies and I got a stack of paper and like six boxes of only green crayons. So, I went to the principal and said, "I think there has been a mistake."
>
> She said, "Yes there has, but there is nothing we can do about it. All the green crayons were sent to our school, all the red crayons were sent somewhere else, there is nothing we can do about it. We just have to make do." So I brought whatever I could from home and started with this group of mainly boys. I had such a hard time, such a hard time. The second week there I got to school one day and my room had been ransacked and all the stuff, including my own boom box, had been stolen. It was a horrible day; all the things I had planned to do I couldn't do because everything was gone. After school that day, I was sitting in the room crying and the janitor came in. I also felt really horrible, like I was not doing any good, and I was not doing anyone any service by doing this job that I did not clearly know how to do. The janitor came in and she said, "You know if you go down the hall, Mr. So and So is crying too and if you go upstairs to Cathy, she was crying yesterday." So that janitor kind of opened the door for me to kind of start talking to other

people about how hard it was and I started that summer to being more honest and to start talking to people.

Talking to people and exploding the myth of being the "only" one, is crucial. This is particularly true for teachers on an anti-racist path. Working against ingrained white supremacy requires action in words and deeds. This, in turn, can create significant alienation from peers.

Resisting Slamming the Classroom Door

Several of the teachers in the study on anti-racist teachers spoke to the push towards isolation as a way to survive. Many of the participants in the study discussed feeling ignored, pushed aside, or silenced as they worked for anti-racist education. Though this invisibility came in a number of forms, it served a common purpose: to marginalize the teachers from the rest of their teaching colleagues and to limit the impact of the work they were able to do beyond their classrooms. Some of the teachers in the study felt like they were only seen when they "played by the rules," which in this case meant not bringing up discussions of race or racism with their colleagues.

Ms. Wilson notes,

> I feel alone. Except my voice isn't alone if I choose to ignore and not bring up anything that is of concern to me in terms of social justice or race, then I can have many conversations that satisfy the people that I work with. But I have burning questions about why we can't talk about issues as history teachers. Why we can't talk about issues that really have had a serious impact on this country, and still do? But, if I simply go along with the agenda of certain people, then I can hang in there and have conversations about gardens just like everybody else. If I play the game, then I can be included because then people think I am thinking like them.

The work of anti-racism is a difficult and painful process, one that involves looking inward and outward. Inclusive anti-racist teachers must examine their own biases and racial socialization. Part of that interior work requires that someone else hold up the mirror to help teachers see themselves. If an anti-racist teacher is isolated, it becomes more difficult to do that work.

Finding a supportive anti-racist community is crucial for anyone seeking to create the conditions necessary for all students to thrive. Another, perhaps more painful reason that white anti-racists must engage in community is that one's biases MUST be challenged.

You Never Asked (or I Never Wanted to Be Named Becky)

As a high school teacher, I obtained a small grant to start a multicultural center in an unused space in the school. The goals of the center were modest: students would have access to some after school programming (African drumming, yoga, rehearsals for Spoken Word competitions, a storytelling clinic, and the like) and the center would be open for tutoring and hanging out before school, after school, and during lunch periods. With the grant money we purchased three computers and a printer. We created a small donation-based library, repainted the room (in a district approved color pallet) and opened our doors. I reached out to a few colleagues and together we worked to staff the center during our free periods and raise awareness that the center existed.

A colleague soon approached us and asked if we would consider sponsoring a group of ninth grade African American girls that were struggling to find community within our school. The evidence of these students not finding a place in the school was clear. Members of this group of around 15 young women could frequently be found sitting outside of classrooms (after having been sent out by a teacher), roaming halls during classes, or getting into fights during lunch periods.

I vaguely knew some of these students, but did not have any of them in class. Another teacher and myself decided to offer a support style group for a select group of African American ninth grade girls (including students identified as struggling). We invited a community elder, a renowned poet and mentor, to come in every Friday during lunch and offer different workshops for the students. We had high hopes and wanted the group to seem special. To that end, my colleague (a former art teacher) designed beautiful invitations and we hand-delivered them to students during their homeroom. (Note that at no point in this process did we ask the students what they wanted or needed.)

We knew we only had a short period of time each week with the students and did not want to waste time for students to get their lunches themselves. However, we did not have the budget to buy lunch for 20 students each week. So, we worked with the head of food services each week. (Most of the girls received free or reduced-price lunch and thus had somewhat limited choices for lunch each day.) Prior to each week's meeting we would get Friday's menu, contact each participant and have her make a lunch choice.

It was a lot of work, to be sure. And as the weeks went on I began to resent the students' constant complaints and demands. One person didn't want the lunch she ordered the previous week. Another demanded ranch dressing. Another wanted to see what else there was to eat and left a meeting. After about 4 weeks of this we noticed that students were not showing up to meetings at all. We would go to the cafeteria and remind students it was Friday and some would join us and others would avoid eye contact and move away.

After one particularly horrible meeting I went home and began to complain loudly to my husband about how ungrateful these students were being. I said, "I am not their servant and they have me running back and forth to the cafeteria to get them a different lunch. I'm doing this for them, and I'm begging them to show up ?!?"

He nodded and then offered a privilege check, "You know for some of those girls choosing their lunch is one of the only choices they get in the school day. It is already a limited choice. Lunch is one of the only free times they have. You took that from them. You didn't really ask if that's what they wanted."

Now the virtuous version of myself would have embraced such feedback. It is doubtful that happened in the moment. But I know I heard his words. I reflected on the roots of the group and the way we went about building it. The idea of the group came from another teacher who wanted something "done about those girls." My impulse was to protect students that had become targets of a lot of ire. As the fall progressed, faculty meetings were full of coded racial signifiers about "those ninth grade girls thinking they own the place." I once witnessed one of the girls wiping her Hot Cheetos' stained fingers along the white walls of the school. I saw desperation in that action: This school is not mine and means less than a napkin to me. I wanted to help. I wanted to protect. And yes, I wanted to save.

But in my savior mode, I neglected to ask what the very students I was trying to "help" wanted. Instead I fell into a paternalistic mode of creating a support group that none of the students asked for, nor had a hand in designing. I did not know most of these students from class. I just knew of them from teachers complaining to me about *them*. As the white lady that talks about race I stepped to the fore, but I didn't do the work needed. I invited an African American community elder that I knew from her work with younger children and did not think of the specific needs of this age group.

Of course, students resented this project. But it wasn't until Steve pointed it out that I understood how the failure of this endeavor was a result of my arrogance and isolation. The support group meetings quickly (or always?) became about *me* helping *those* students. I became the center of the action. I had lost the humility, empathy, and critical consciousness required of an inclusive anti-racist educator. I am grateful for Steve's perceptiveness and that we are close enough that he could point out my privilege and lack of insight. But, the truth is, had I been less isolated and less enamored of my own work I would have seen this folly much earlier. I would have likely avoided some of the wasted time and increased alienation for the students I had set out to "help." Further, had I taken the time to *talk to the students and listen to their experiences,* a more inclusive community could have resulted.

I was able to see the discrimination these young women were experiencing and understood to an extent why these students might feel alienated at the school, *but I never asked students specifically.* I relied on my own conceptions of myself being a "with it" white person. A bit of humility and a lot of listening could have alleviated many of these problems. Luckily there was enough time left in the academic year to change courses. We ditched the mandatory lunch meetings, but offered the space every Friday lunch nonetheless. The students eventually claimed the lunchtime spot, laughing, talking, and enjoying each other's company. There was no preset programming, just a space that was held especially for these students. It was the need to be seen, to have a space carved out that let these young women know that they mattered in a school.

In addition to individual growth and catching one's own limited world view, there is a desperate need for community in order to sustain change at an institutional level over time. Sustainable change cannot take place if it is placed at the feet of and picked up by *one* person. (To explore ways that power and dominance can negatively impact pedagogy see Appendix G: "There is More than One Way to Tell this Story.")

Deliberate Community

Much has been written about the isolation of teaching. Researchers examining the lives of teachers have found that teaching is marked by physical and intellectual separation from colleagues (i.e., Little, 1990). There is a cost to all when there is no learning community for teachers.

Even though I and other anti-racist teachers I've studied understand the importance of having a supportive community in which to grow as anti-racist teachers, daily interactions with colleagues make finding such community difficult.

Palmer (1998) stresses the concept of "living divided no more" in his call for teacher renewal. While I do not think the teachers in my study of anti-racist teachers were divided regarding their anti-racist focus, many felt that there was a disconnect between their individual passion for anti-racist social justice and the reality of working in institutions that did not share that passion. As a result, they divided their lives into putting everything they had into the anti-racist work in school and seeking the fuel for that from outside sources and their students. To continue to foster and develop inclusive anti-racist educators, we need to build communities within schools that deliberately, publicly, and systematically find ways to support the growth of such teachers (and students).

The first step toward creating such sustaining communities is to very deliberately declare one's passion and ideals around anti-racism. The "deliberate community" specifically seeks to build allies around the concept of anti-racism and sustains the group members' work while challenging each other and the status quo. Nieto (2004) writes of the importance of pushing beyond the sometimes-seductive power of going it alone:

> The image of the teacher as a knight on a white horse is hopelessly romantic and, at the same time, ultimately defeating, because it is an illusion that takes too much energy to sustain. I suggest instead that a far more promising approach is to build collaborative relationships.... This means that teachers need to go into the teachers' room, but they must learn to talk with, learn from, and challenge their colleagues in a consistent and constructive manner that reinforces teachers and learners. (p. 397)

For inclusive anti-racist teachers to be effective beyond the classroom, we must push beyond the feelings of being the "only one" and disregard the sanctions from colleagues that attack anti-racist work. Crucial to this deliberate community is placing the goals of anti-racism in the center of the community. Everything from curriculum to extra-curricular activities to staffing to tardy policies to tracking patterns must be viewed through the inclusive anti-racist lens.

Forming such groups can take many forms, from book groups, to lunch gatherings to invitations to visit one another's classrooms or co-create lessons. I know one principal whose entire professional development model works for inclusive racial justice. Within that she offers a number of different paths that teachers can take to engage the work. She does not assume that everyone is at the same place in terms of examining their own biases and privileges. Instead of shaming some teachers or promoting others as having "finished the work" she provides different readings, workshops, book and study groups, that can engage people while pushing them to find new avenues to realize inclusive anti-racist work.

While whole school *deliberately anti-racist communities (DAC)* may be ideal, it isn't always possible. Starting small, even within a teaching team or a department can provide much needed support. The important issue is that the group keeps inclusive anti-racism as the focus. The group can move forward on several fronts. First, the community offers support for the continued growth of inclusive anti-racist teachers. This can take the form of looking at each other's lesson plans, planning units, watching each other teach or team teaching. It can be a shared reading that teachers journal about or volunteering to speak as a team at a faculty meeting.

A group of my teaching colleagues at my former high school (my DAC) once decided to invite people to anonymously submit stories about foundational lessons they have learned about race in their lives. We then put those stories into a reader's theater format and performed them for a faculty in-service. We designed follow-up questions for the faculty to respond to what they heard and saw. Both the preparation and reflection on the pieces within our DAC and the follow-up conversations with the rest of the faculty were powerful and opened up space for many to engage in deep reflection.

There is no set formula and no exam that one can take to "pass" as a certified inclusive anti-racist teacher. All teachers who commit to using the lens of anti-racism as the guiding principle in our lives must continually work to achieve this goal and must acknowledge when we fall short of this goal. The DAC can help teachers discover ways they fall short of the goals while supporting and building on the positive work they do. Hooks (2003) remarks, "to build community requires vigilant awareness of the work we must continually do to undermine all the socialization that leads us to behave in ways that perpetuate domination" (p. 36).

The inclusive anti-racist educator makes normal what the dominant worldviews as abnormal. Normal behavior then means challenging others regarding racist acts, it may mean speaking out at department or faculty meetings again and again about racial inequity, it may mean restructuring a curriculum long held as the norm. However, within a group that is deliberately constructed around inclusive anti-racist teaching, the behavior that has been marginalized by the dominant group is embraced as normal and necessary.

While a crucial element to building and sustaining inclusive anti-racist teachers is a deliberate community around the common goal of anti-racism, the work must extend beyond a small group and reach into the larger community of the schools in which we work. I firmly believe we need a strong community of support to do this work. However, if the work begins and ends with conversations and reflections amongst inclusive anti-racist teachers, there is no agitating for wider change and limited opportunities for others to change. Palmer (1998) is helpful in describing the importance of a larger community: "When we talk to each other, and not to a larger audience, no movement can emerge—and we are more likely to fall into delusion and error" (p. 175).

At the center of inclusive anti-racist work is the hope that things can change. To foster that hope we must believe that teachers can change. One of the most difficult tasks of the inclusive anti-racist educator may be welcoming opportunities to engage teachers who may operate outside the anti-racist agenda. This is one area where white anti-racist teachers especially need to step up to the plate. It is too much to ask and to expect colleagues of color to continually educate well-meaning white people. Other white teachers need to stand up to the challenge of pushing white teachers from a space of non-racist to actively anti-racist.

I started the discussion of DAC with a reference to living divided no longer, translated essentially as putting one's ideals into action in all areas of life. I fundamentally believe in the worth and dignity of every person. While on the surface, this meaning may seem obvious, however, it becomes much more difficult when faced with someone with whom you strongly disagree or who is doing damage to students. In the case of my own anti-racist work, I have tended to demonize certain colleagues because of their racist actions towards students or their behavior during some of the anti-racist workshops. Such demonization has led me to believe that such people will never change and that my time is wasted in attempting to engage them in anti-racist conversation. Hooks (2003) helps remind me of the danger of this kind of thinking:

> Whenever we love justice and stand on the side of justice we refuse simplistic binaries. We refuse to allow either/or thinking to cloud our judgment. We embrace both/and. We acknowledge the limits of what we know. (p. 10)

Within the DAC, I envision and versions I have participated in, the either/or thinking I described above is mitigated. I must avoid such binary thinking not only because it divides me from a spiritual principle I have accepted as a Truth in my life, but also because it undermines my ability to work for change.

My vision of the DAC could provide a safeguard from this kind of thinking. The community can support members as we seek to discover new allies and hear from those who think we are simply self-righteous or offtrack. Community members are also pushed to challenge others rather than remain in the safety of the known community. Additionally, the DAC will help members to perceive the dedication of teachers who, for whatever reason, have not focused on anti-racist agendas in their teaching. We cannot become so insular or so self-assured that we assume we have nothing to learn.

The ideal DAC supports us in our endeavors to both learn and teach. In order to continue this work, we must believe in the potential for people (ourselves included) to change. Again, hooks (2003) offers a vision of hope for change:

> While it is a truism that every citizen of this nation, white or colored, is born into a racist society that attempts to socialize us from the moment of our birth to accept the tenets of white supremacy, it is equally true that we can choose to resist this socialization. (p. 56)

The deliberate community acknowledges that we are working against the racist socialization. We must invite others in and support each other as we fight and choose against racism and towards a more inclusive and just society.

More than ever I believe we need to work together. Going it alone is costly and scary. Whether it is shutting the classroom door to insulate oneself from institutional racism and serve as a "hero" teacher or a lone political protest—without community, the power of the work is lost. The chance for growth is limited. One must not wait for popular approval to stand up against hate, but without reflection, solo acts inflate the power of one. In acting solo, I can neglect to see the work of others or that resistance is possible *because* of others, not in spite of them. As I replay the actions of my work throughout my career I realize that so much has been honed in that classroom years ago when I stood up to the basketball star and was mocked by my teacher. So much of me leans to going it alone.

Where I am from tells me that I must fight racism. My roots in that small central Illinois town tell me that I will likely be one of a few white people doing this. And for that I will stand out as different and odd. My history tells me to resist racism *alone*. But that isn't sustainable and ignores the wisdom of others and obscures the work I still have to do in myself. Where I must travel is through the fog of isolation and exceptionalism to a community in which we all work towards a just inclusive and anti-racist world. This book is a step through that fog—a step towards that hope.

Activities Related to Introduction

How's My School or District Doing?

Background: In April of 2018, The U.S. Department of Education's Office of Civil Rights released data that demonstrate patterns of inequity and injustice in schools and districts across the country. This activity asks participants to examine their own school or district and explore the material impact of various policies and procedures on students.

Activity

1. Go to https://ocrdata.ed.gov/DistrictSchoolSearch. Lookup the most recent year of data available for a school and/or school district of interest to you. If a specific school doesn't come up do a search for the district.

   – On the right of the screen for each report there is a blue grey box entitled, "Special Reports and Other Profile Facts." Click on the "Discipline Report" which will provide you with data on which groups of students a school or district is most likely to suspend, expel, and refer to law enforcement. You can also see who's more likely to be arrested at school using the "School Related Arrests" tab. You can also look at the "Educational Equity Report" to see who has access to college prep/AP courses, and more.

2. Take notes on what you see. Notice the intersection of race, disability, gender, SES. Consider the following questions:

   – What surprises you here?/What patterns do you notice?
   – Who has access to high quality curricula?
   – What does the data tell about experiences of students with disabilities?
   – Who is being pushed out?
   – Who is not there? Why?
   – How do you make sense of this data?
   – How can you keep from abstracting this to being someone else's problem?
   – What role might you play in creating these patterns?
   – What role can you play in disrupting these patterns?

APPENDIX B

Activities Related to Chapter 1

Reflective Activities on the Stories of Race
"Danger of a Single Story"

Background: Watch "Chimamanda Adichie—The Danger of a Single Story" (Adichie, 2009).

Reflection: Have participants take a sheet of paper and fold it into four equal sections. They will respond to each prompt on a separate quarter of the paper.

Respond in writing and/or drawings to these four prompts:

- What are the various stories that have shaped your understanding of race?
- When did you first become aware of yourself as a member of a racial group?
- Is it difficult to talk about race? Why or why not? In what situations do you feel the most comfortable?
- A single story about your identity might be ...

Process: Depending on the needs and the size of the group there are several different ways to process this activity. I describe two processing approaches can be used for any variety of discussion prompts. I will describe other prompts and approaches for other activities. But these can be adapted to fit a number of different topics.

A. Talking Wheel

Set Up

Determine what works best for the size of the group, the space available and the needs of participants. For example, if there is group member for whom it may be difficult to move, choose a set up option that accommodates that need. Also, be aware of other inclusive needs, such as those that might have difficult hearing when multiple conversations are happening.

> *Standing option:* Have participants form two concentric circles. The inner circle faces outward and the outward circle faces inward.
> *Seated option with chairs:* Have participants form two concentric circles with chairs. The inner circle faces outward the outward circle faces inward.
> *Seated option with desks:* Have participants form two lines of desks facing each other.

Process

After you have determined the method and set up the room that works best for the group, declare one circle A and the other B. Then ask one group to go first. Read the prompt you wish them to discuss and set a time for them to talk while the other partner listens. Stop, then have the other group talk about the prompt. After both groups A and B have spoken, PAUSE. Ask participants to discuss with each other what they were comfortable sharing. After the facilitator has processed the prompt, the outside circle moves one to the left and the inside circle stays put. This continues through four cycles.

Facilitator Role

Between each prompt, pause the discussion and step into the middle of the circle or somewhere where everyone can see you. Ask participants if there is anything they would like to share with the larger group.

IMPORTANT: Partners must share their own stories and not share their partner's without the partner's prior approval.

Caution: Often in multiracial groups where white students have not had many opportunities to talk about their own race, they (white students) will tell the story of their partner if the partner is a student of color. If this happens remind participants that this is about discovering one's own stories about race. It is crucial that in working towards anti-racist communities, students of color are not sacrificed to the learning of white students. This holds true for learners of all ages.

Rationale for This Exercise

As I argue throughout the book, it is crucial for anti-racist educators to determine the stories we have consumed that have shaped our understandings about race. Since we consume racialized images and ideas with our daily oatmeal, we have to pause and consider the impact of these. This exercise allows one to do so without the shame and blame. The talking wheel allows for a quick check in with a partner and allows for some rapid-fire honesty. There is some safety in knowing you will rotate and that the facilitator is also there to help process what is shared.

B. Knee to Knee

Set Up

Each member of the group finds or is assigned a partner. Partners turn desks or chairs to face one another. Ideally, the two people are sitting close enough to almost be touching knee to knee. However, it is important to remember that not all bodies are "typical" and any physical arrangement must be inclusive. Therefore, the facilitator should be prepared to change the physical set up so all are included and no one is singled out. (This means change the activity for all so that all are included rather than saying to the one group that cannot touch "you don't have to do this part.")

Process

The facilitator reads one of the prompts. The two partners take turns responding to prompt and sharing writing. As with discussion wheel, the facilitator takes the time between prompt to ask for responses to share with the larger group.

Rationale for This Exercise

There is power in holding space for another person to tell their own story in the way they wish to tell it. Facing another person and, if possible, making physical contact with them is one way of communicating that they are held and that their worlds matter.

Racial Autobiography and Lessons Along the Way

Preparation: If this is to be shared in a group or in a class, provide a written prompt to the class members before this session. This is a more formal and thorough approach to writing about the stories we are told about race. Additionally, this is a chance for individuals to assess the types of knowledge they have been exposed to throughout their education.

Prompt: Consider the foundational stories in your life regarding race and racial identity. The following questions are ones to consider, but you need not answer all of them. What were you taught about race? How were you taught to see yourself? Consider how these lessons may have shaped your understandings and how you approach your own teaching. In your opinion, how much does racism impact what happens in schools? What would you like to know more about? How do you relate to students who do not appear to match your racial identity? What worries you the most in regards to discussions of race? In what ways do considerations of race, racism, or racial identity impact the choices you make in the classroom?

Alternative or Additional Prompt: Consider your racial literacy and important influences in your thinking. Set a timer for 5 minutes. Make a list of significant books, authors, thinkers, and teachers that have stuck with you over time and who have helped you understand the world. When the timer is up, look at the list and see who is there and who might not be there. Consider what sorts of knowledge you have been exposed to throughout your education. What areas are missing? Who is privileged in your list? How has your thinking been shaped by this?

Alternative or Additional Prompt: Go to http://sundown.tougaloo.edu/sundowntowns.php and explore the history of your town or towns near your home. What were some of the laws and customs that dictated racial segregation and formal and informal policies? If your town is listed as a sundown town what is your reaction? Does this surprise you? Upset you? How might have this influenced your own education? Your family's? Your teachers?

Process: Again I offer two different options for processing this activity. These options could be used in many different ways.

A. *Gallery*

Set Up

   Provide participants with newsprint, markers, crayons, and so on.

Prepare

Ask participants to use the newsprint to make a visual representation of their autobiography. Encourage them to use a combination of quotes and pictures to capture some of the key ideas in their work. When everyone is finished, post these around the room.

Individual Reaction

Give everyone in the room sticky notes. Have them walk around the room and respond to what they see by writing on a sticky note and attaching it to the paper. Also invite participants to use the sticky notes to make notes to themselves that they wish to share with the larger group.

Group Reaction

Bring group back together to discuss what was there. Find areas of commonality and difference. Be sure to honor who is in the room. When the session is over, invite participants to take posters and comments with them and amend their autobiographies if the comments and conversation pushed them to think of something new.

Rationale for This Exercise

It can be daunting to share writing in a group setting. Further, asking individuals to move from strictly written to more symbolic forms of representations pushes them to consider more ways to understand and represent their thinking and teaching. People walk around the room and react to the posters. This approach allows more people to comment beyond sharing in a large group. Additionally, each group member walks away with the reactions without being put on the spot and can take time to reflect in private.

━━━━

That's Not What I Said

Set Up

Have participants sit facing one another.

Prompt

Facilitator offers a general prompt based on the racial autobiography.

Respond

One person responds to the prompt and the other listens.

Recall

The listener repeats back what they heard. The responder then gets to correct anything that wasn't accurate or misrepresented what they said.

This process continues until the first person that spoke is satisfied that they had been heard and understood. The process is then repeated for the second person.

Rationale for This Exercise

Too often people hear what makes them most comfortable and included. This is especially true for those who have grown up practicing nice white talk and had their white fragility protected. In this kind of talk a form of false empathy takes place, especially when one is confronted with a story that illustrates white racism and supremacy. This exercise forces all listeners to realize their own listening biases and to fully focus on what the person across from them is saying.

Activities Related to Chapter 2

Fire in the Belly: An Exercise in Several Parts

The following exercise is a version of an activity I have done a number of different ways and have observed this or read about it in different places over the years. I first witnessed it while observing a former teaching colleague, Tracy Wagner. Years later, after I had done a variety of iterations for a variety of audiences, I came across a version of the exercise written up by Linda Christensen of *Rethinking Schools*. I state this here because the work of inclusive anti-racist teaching requires that we build on each other's work while acknowledging (whenever possible) the work that went before us (or that was happening simultaneously or without our knowledge).

Naming the Fire in the Belly

Background: Read Margaret Walker's poem "For My People"

Refection (prewriting): Jot down what you see as the most important aspects of your job as a teacher. Look at the list then reflect (through writing or just silent reflection):

- Why these things and not others?
- What fuels these goals?
- What personal beliefs, spiritual practices, or other teachings shape the ways you view the world and your teachings?
- What teachings, teachers, or others are significant in the way your worldview has taken shape and your view of teaching?

Next: Consider the biggest challenges you face in teaching (or if a preservice teacher what concerns do you have as you prepare to teach). Where do you find yourself reaching to for comfort or as you face these challenges?

Reflection (Reading): Set aside your freewrite for now. Read or reread the poem, "For My People."

Reflection (Writing): Using the Walker piece for your inspiration, create your own poem. Consider who your people are, (does it include a world with your students?), consider what you most value and what you hope to stand for in the world. If it is helpful you can substitute the phrase "For my students." Below are sample stanzas from preservice teachers working in an urban teaching internship. Some students requested to include their names in this section and others opted not to be identified. I have honored their requests.

Example 1: by Chelsea Colby (used with permission)

For my people struggling with those they loved
Alcohol and anger and slurring and stumbling
Judgement and disapproval
Driving and fear
Cleaning—and making a mess
Detachment and protection and sadness and love

For my people in the woods
Seeking solace from the chaos
The chaos from the world
And the chaos that is ourselves
Remember you are not where you come from

and you are not your parents
And yet they shape you
and from the community you are not separate

For my people who walk this world as a woman
May you find the strength to stand up for yourself
And not to apologize for existing, for taking up space,
For breathing and speaking and thinking and fighting
Keep fighting
Everything is political
Your body is not neutral

Example 2: by Oliver Wijayapala (used with permission)

For my people,
The neglected children who struggle living in the city and country of San Francisco
The children hidden from tourist brochures and newspaper articles
The children of diversity, but finding an unknown ground, pride, and identity with others within its 49 square miles.

For the young man afraid to walk in his own neighborhood, who spits at the color blue, who's scared to wear red, who hates seeing red and blue in the distance: the men in blue making the color red.

For the child of Filipino immigrants struggling to find a job or two after school, hoping to actualize the American dream that her parents failed to obtain

For all the other children, whose voices are silence and stories untold,
that wake up in the morning fog
with heavy hearts
but hope to begin their life anew.

Example 3: (name withheld at student request)

For my people, learning to make a habit out of loving those they do not know.
Fighting reflexes and TV dinner first impressions—bland, simplified, and salty.

For my people, the kids who got bored because the bar was set too
high or too low

and then used to beat them into reaching for something they weren't
sure that mattered.

For those who proved over and over that teaching to the middle is a
recipe for teaching almost no one.

For my people.

Get out of your seats, drop the crossword puzzles, run in the hallways,
demand recess, chew gum

Say ain't, say ya'all, say bro—say your book report in an accent that
doesn't choke you.

Recognize that weird works, that different is not a synonym for impossible

and that connection is as essential as it is unavoidable.

May we have the courage to listen

May we have the courage to teach

Example 4: by Sarah Vandiver Koch (used with permission)

For my students, who I am sure cannot be imagined in one stanza,

but who will fill classrooms and communities with thinking,

critiquing, creating, talking, sharing, laughing, reading, and writing,
engaging, playing, jumping, sitting, standing, listening, singing,
acting, resisting, insisting, believing, and knowing.

Processing: Like the previous chapter, there are several ways to process this
activity. The first step is individual regardless of whether this activity is done
alone or in a group.

Individual reflection: Go back to your prewriting list regarding what you
cared about in your teaching. Consider the following questions:

- How much of that showed up in your "for my people" poem?
- Is there a disconnect between your role as a teacher and how you
  view the world?
- Who are your people? Do you envision them as part of your class-
  room and school community or separate from that?
- What does the poem most reveal about you and what you stand for?

Optional individual reflection: Read the sample selections for student poems and think about the connections and the possible contradictions they

represent. Think about how these visions of community, self, and people might be translated to classroom practice.

Group Reflection: If you are doing this exercise as part of a class or group sharing all or part of the poems with each other can be a very important tool to help people talk about the fire in the belly. I recommend the following as one of the more inclusive ways to process the poems.

1. If possible, have the group members e-mail you their poems or whatever portions of their poems they are comfortable sharing prior to the class or the workshop.
2. The teacher or facilitator makes large print copies of the poem and makes enough copies for everyone in the class or workshop (If you are unable to make copies due to resources or time constraints, I suggest having newsprint and markers available and inviting students to write portions of their poems large enough for others to see.)
3. Assemble the group to read aloud portions of their poems that they are comfortable sharing. If other participants have copies of the poems, invite them to follow along as the person reads and high-light words or phrases that stand out or resonate with the listener in some way. If possible, have the poems emerge organically with silences in between as the next poem emerges. This may make for what seem like long silences, but ultimately this allows for more voices to be heard.

Note: Not all participants must share their poems. Also provide the option of having designated readers for poems that may want to put their poem in the room but may not want to read. Please be aware of the pacing and volume of the reading. Mumbling or racing through the reading in a low voice bars access to many in the room.

1. Once everyone who wants to read has finished, invite the group to write or reflect on what they notice in the poems.
2. Depending on time, needs, and space of the group, the next steps can be an open discussion or a visual map followed by a discussion.
3. For the visual map . . . invite participants to come to the chalk board, white board, or provide newsprint and write down words or phrases that stood out to them. Participants should be encouraged to move around to different spaces on the various writing spaces. Once that is finished, again depending on the setup, participants can do a gallery walk (described in Appendix B) or step back and see the finished work.

4. Now ask participants to note the connections and themes they see in the work on the board and begin translating this to the core ideas that fuel our "Fire in the Belly" and the work we do in the classroom. Depending on the class this may be a time to introduce some readings and discuss theoretical lenses that expand and build on notions of community and anti-racist inclusive practice.

Activities Related to Chapter 3

Reflective Activities on Inclusive Practices
This is What They Notice

This exercise can be another useful tool for educators to understand the different ways students' identities are ignored or celebrated in the classroom.

Setup: On a piece of paper ask participants to list all of the ways that they identify. These can include race, gender, disability, but also roles they play in life . . . sister, daughter, mother, athlete, and so forth.

Process: Ask participants to circle the categories that are most important to them. Then ask them to star the ones that are most noticed, remarked upon, or otherwise seem important to teachers in class.

Group Discussion: Where are the differences in these lists? Why are some aspects of identity notice and others ignored in school? What aspects of identity seem most important to note and in what ways should those be noticed?

I Want to Belong

...as soon as we take away a students' sense of belonging, we completely undermine their capacity to learn the skills that will enable them to belong. Herein lies the most painful "catch-22" situation that confronts students with disabilities—they can't belong until they learn, but they can't learn because they are prevented from belonging.

—Norman Kunc (as quoted in Villa & Thousand, 2005, p. 45)

This exercise is a brief way to help students and teachers alike conceive of the importance of inclusion. And though the quote above references students with disabilities it is crucial to consider all of the ways we tell students they don't belong: through race, class, gender, and language. And what mechanisms (suspensions, expulsions, limited Eurocentric curricula, narrow pedagogical approaches) are used to tell students they do not belong.

Setup: The facilitator passes out blank paper and pens, pencils, crayons, and markers to participants and then invites participants to close their eyes.

Round 1: The facilitator then asks participants to think of a time that they felt like they belonged and were included in learning. This learning could be in a formal setting like school, on a team, or other extracurricular activity or other informal learning done within a family (i.e., a grandparent teaching a grandchild how to cook a specific dish unique to the family).

Ask participants to:
– Picture the details of the situation...Ask: Where did this take place? What did it look like? How old were you? Who was with you? What were you learning? What was happening to help you feel a sense of belonging?
– Recall how you felt and reacted: How did you feel? What did you share with others? How did you feel about those around you? Did you feel about yourself?

Action: Have participants open eyes and write, draw, or otherwise chronicle what they recalled about belonging.

Round 2: Invite participants to close their eyes again. This time ask them to picture a time in learning where they felt ostracized. A time that they felt distinctly out of place and not included. Repeat the same prompts as before. Recall the details of situation and how you felt.

Action: Have participants open eyes and write, draw, or otherwise chronicle what they recalled about belonging.

Reflection: Invite participants to share their stories and drawings in small groups or pairs. Once people have had a chance to share ask them to find commonalities about what actions were taken to help them belong. Ask them to share the difference between feeling included and feeling excluded. Invite them to think of teachers or classmates that might feel excluded from learning and brainstorm ways to invite them into the learning.

But This Student Is . . .

This exercise is designed to help teachers "flip the script" on deficit thinking and instead work from the strengths of a student. This warm-up activity leads directly into a longer student learning profile activity.

Setup: Pass out paper and ask participants to fold it in half.

Action Round 1: Ask participants to think of a student that is a challenging for them. Set a timer for 1 minute. On the right hand side of the paper ask participants to make a list of the behaviors and descriptors that describe that student. (They only have 1 minute to do this.)

Reflection: Ask participants to look at their lists. Invite them to pay attention to the language they used to describe the students. Have them circle anything that falls into a deficit-model framing of the student (i.e., bossy, apathetic, always argues about wearing headphones . . .).

Action Round 2: Returning to Causton and Tracy-Bronson's (2015)—mentioned in the chapter (3)—question posing approach to changing the way we talk and think about students ask yourself, "What can this student do? What are this person's talents? How would a parent (or guardian) who deeply loves this student speak about him or her?" (p. 57). Return to the piece of paper and on the left hand side of the paper ask participants to reframe the way they think and write about the student. Ask them to list the gifts, talents, strengths, and interests of the student (i.e., creativity is fueled by music, likes to have opportunities to lead a group, sometimes needs a direct invitation to join activities).

Reflection: Lead a discussion on the difference in the two lists and how reframing how we think about students might open up more opportunities to include and engage students. It also might be a chance for participants to look at the areas of bias in their own teaching and approach to students and seek support for working against that bias.

Learning Profile

This activity can support teachers in continuing to build a strength-based approach to all students. I have included the activity as I use it in my "Models of Inclusive Education" course but, like all activities in this book, there are many ways to vary the activity.

Setup: Provide participants with a scenario that describes a child. Whenever possible it should be a child the teachers do not currently teach. I have found it is fun to use a lightly fictionalized version of my own learning profile as a child. After reading the profile ask teachers to complete the chart listed at the end of the example.

Process: Ask teachers to discuss what deficit language was present in the scenario and what they did to find the strengths of the student.

Going Deeper: Have participants write their own scenarios modeled after the example here or another one the facilitator creates. Have colleagues point out the strengths they see in each other's learning styles and so on. Then have teachers apply the same activity to an actual student who presents challenges to them in class. As teachers write up the scenarios, invite them to interrogate any biases that appear especially as they apply to cultural, racial, ability, or language differences between the child and the teacher.

Alternative: Have teachers complete a learning profile (listed at the end of the scenario) for a student in their class.

Sample Student Scenario

Tara is a white, nondisabled, 8-year-old girl. She is one of 4 siblings all of whom have attended or will attend this school. Her parents both work outside the home. Tara usually brings lunch from home, but is eligible for our reduced-price lunch program. Tara comes to class each day clean and dressed appropriately for the day's activities (with the exception of gender issues, which we will discuss later.)

Though she is mostly compliant in class, she often seems to be in her own world. She is frequently frustrated when she does not have time to complete a game or finish a story or drawing. Tara may have trouble distinguishing real life from pretend: She once told a story about invisible horses living in her garage. She is drawn to role-playing activities and will frequently work to engage other students in her pretend games. This sometimes results in her isolation from peers.

She enjoys moving her body, but in both her fine and gross motor skills she lags behind her peers. In our square dancing unit, she continually confused left and right and stepped on many classmates in the process. She will also make up elaborate reasons that she cannot go to gym class simply because she does not yet tie her shoes consistently and would rather avoid changing into her gym shoes because she has to tie them.

Additionally, Tara is overly-attached to adults and attempts to befriend them (whether they be teachers, aides, or lunch staff) in social groups and activities. She can frequently be found bothering the adults during playground duty by standing near them, rather than engaging with her peers. When asked to go play she claims she doesn't like the games the girls are playing.

Further, she has an unrealistic conception of fairness. She can be moved to tears if she witnesses one of her classmates being treated poorly. This has had an impact on the class practice of spelling tests. Our class has a spelling tree, each week, any student that receives 100% on the spelling test has a leaf attached to the tree. Those that do receive 100 on the spelling test have leaves placed at the base of the tree. Recently, Tara started to miss words she had previously spelled correctly. When asked about it she said, "Well, Todd isn't on the tree yet."

Tara also has some gender confusion issues. She refuses to wear dresses and insists on wearing a St. Louis Cardinals baseball cap at all times. She recently came to school with short hair (something that many teachers were disappointed in because her long hair was so pretty). She once tricked a playground aid into thinking she was a boy and went to the boys' side of the playground for lunch recess. We talked to her about how lying is not a school or community value.

At this point we are also concerned with Tara's computational skills. As her summer school teacher noted, "Tara can't do math." We have noted that she is especially thrown by timed math tests and her number facts are nearly nonexistent. In summary:

- Reads at grade level (but prefers stories to facts);
- below grade level in math skills;
- social development uneven;
- plays immature games often/but also wants attention and approval of adults/can engage adults in conversation;
- constantly wants to negotiate rules around issues of fairness, sometimes picked last in games that involve hand/eye coordination, and frequently avoids playing with same-aged female peers;
- development delayed in fine and gross motor skills;
- inappropriate expression of gender; and
- has difficulty following classroom procedures, especially related to timed tasks and order.

Suggested Learning Profile

This can be a powerful tool to help reframe beliefs about students and confront biases.

- **Name of student:**
- **Age:**
- **Demographic information** (race, gender identity, SES, disability status, family structure):

- **Narrative profile:** Write a paragraph that someone who does not know the student could read to get a better understanding of who this child is and what knowledge and gifts they bring to the classroom community.

- **How do parents or guardians describe the student?**

- **Strengths and likes in school:**

- **Areas of interest outside of school:**

- **Areas in need of support:**

- **One positive aspect of this student** that you as the teacher wants to especially note and build upon as part of the student's success in the class (and that you will help the student see in themselves):

Activities Related to Chapter 4

Reflective Activities on Discussions of Race and Difference

Sticky Note Notions

This is a general activity I use following a particularly challenging or provocative reading or film. For example, I have used this with a variety of groups to help process the concept of white privilege and white supremacy after reading Peggy McIntosh's (1989) "White Privilege: Unpacking the Invisible Knapsack" alongside Zeus Leonardo's (2004) "The Color of Supremacy: Beyond the Discourse of 'White Privilege'" (both are listed in the References).

> **Setup:** Provide participants with three different colored sticky notes. Around the room have posted the categories...
>
> AGREE   DISAGREE   WONDER ABOUT
>
> **Prepare:** Have participants write down one idea from the reading or film that they agreed with, one they disagreed with, and one they

---

Through the Fog, pages 147–150

are still wondering about. Have participants post these around the room under the appropriate categories.

(*Access note:* Ask students to print firmly and write in slightly larger letters. Giving them larger sticky notes might help this. Also, volunteer to scribe for anyone who might not be able to write by hand.)

Individual Process: Ask students to move around the room and find one sticky note they agree with, one they disagree with, and one they wonder about. These can come from any category. In other words, someone might find something in the agree category disagree with. Once they have collected three notes, they return to their seats.

(*Access note:* Spread the Agree/Disagree/Wonder About categories throughout the room so there are not too many people clustered in one section. Also, if there are students for whom moving around the classroom poses a problem, place the sticky notes on newsprint and place them in central locations that people can access without standing.)

Group Process: Have participants share what they found and lead a discussion around the issues that arise.

Rationale: Because of fear, nice white talk, and lack of opportunities to practice engaging in meaningful dialogue about race, large group discussions can often feel stilted, scripted, and often end up silencing many in the room. This can result in replicating the same dominant narrative around race and reinforce stereotypes and racial biases. The sticky note exercise offers a chance to express opinions that others can see and react to without those opinions being immediately connected to a person. It is a chance to examine how a group of people can read or see the same material and take away very different things from it. It is also a chance to practice disagreeing in ways that allow each side to be understood.

Take My Perspective

The prompt for this is similar to the sticky note idea. In this case, participants are asked to respond to a statement. For example, "Teaching is a political act." The prompt ideally will build on prior knowledge and should provoke different responses.

Setup: Provide all participants with a notecard. Give participants a prompt to react to and then provide time for them to write a clear response on their notecard.

Small Group Reaction: Have participants move around the room and then call out a number between 2–4. Participants then get in a group that responds to the number called out. (For example, if the facilitator yells 2, people pair up.) In those groups people read their responses to each other and then switch cards. The game continues with people taking different ideas as their own and representing them to other groups.

Large Group Process: For this, bring the group back together and discuss the ideas that were out there, but for this one also discuss what it felt like to represent an idea that was not your own.

Rationale: Again, because racial talk can become coded and racism slips into conversation in many ways, it is important to realize what one's words may mean to others and how those words are understood. Additionally, taking on another's point of view is important in terms of pushing each other past discomfort and re-alizing that there might be ideas that we had not considered. The calling out of numbers and taking on different personas also can cut tension and allow people to engage in the discussion without being so guarded.

Agree/Disagree Line

I have participated in, and have led this activity under lots of different names and I am not sure where it originated so I use this generic name for it here. Essentially the activity invites participants to take a position and explain it as different statements are read.

Setup: Depending on the size of the group everyone can participate or select members of the class can participate while the larger group watches and then discusses. Across the front of the room place the categories:

Strongly Agree Agree   Disagree   Strongly Disagree

Activity: The facilitator reads a statement. For example, "It is okay to tell racial jokes within groups where everyone is the same race." Participants then move along the line so they line up with the ranking that best matches what they think on this topic.

Group Process: The facilitator invites participants to explain why they chose to stand in this location. If there is a larger group, watching the facilitator invites them to react as well. (In very large groups one can hand out agree/disagree signs and ask the larger group to hold up the sign and respond to the prompt.)

Rationale for this Activity: This is another chance for people to consider differing opinions and explain their viewpoints. Often this reveals areas of bias or areas that individuals may need support on to go further. There is a chance to participate at the level one is most comfortable doing and even if one is sitting quietly, they can consider where they would place themselves and why they might do so.

Activities Related to Chapter 5

My Identity in School

This activity (and the following one) can be a good wake-up call for educators to consider what assumptions we make regarding students' identity. Ideally, like all activities, I recommend educators do this themselves and process with a group before trying this with students.

> **Setup:** Provide each participant with a large sheet of newsprint and markers.
>
> **Individual Reflection:** Ask participants to draw the outline of a body.
>
> – *On the outside of the body* ask participants to list the ways they identify or are identified. (These may include race, gender, sexuality, disability, religion, SES, family structure, nationality, and so forth.) Near each of those identifiers write messages, assumptions, stereotypes about you that are based on these identifiers.

      – *On the inside of the body* ask participants to write down some of the ways these assumptions impact interactions with others. Also ask participants to list messages they wish were part of the story regarding their perceived identity.

Group Reflection: Post the drawings around the room and ask participants to take a walk and note what they see. Bring observations back to the group and discuss commonalities and differences. Ask what surprised people and what was difficult to share.

Caution: Activities like this can put an unfair burden on students who have been historically marginalized by various forms of systemic oppression. This is especially true in predominantly white settings where there may be only a handful of students of color. Because of this, I ask students to put their names on their posters (that way everyone at least is revealed from the start rather than the one student that puts Black down as an identity.) Also while all of us can feel that we are misunderstood and stereotyped, some biases carry more material costs than others.

    For example, when I do this exercise at my present college, white women from the Eastern United States often put that people assume they are rich and that they are clueless. While that is painful, it is not the same as the systemic racism faced by students of color or the danger of revealing a non-apparent marginalized identity (such as disability.) It is up to the facilitator to help participants make distinctions and appreciate the differing costs of assumptions and stereotypes.

Activities Related to Chapter 6

There Is More Than One Way to Tell This Story

This activity can help students and teachers examine patterns of dominance.

> **Setup:** Participants get in groups of three. Ask one person to volunteer to be the referee.
>
> **Activity:** Provide group with prompt to discuss. This can be anything, but should be a topic that can have wide ranging opinions, such as, "React to the statement: Teaching is a political act" or "You can recognize a person's social class by how they speak." Tell participants that they will be discussing the prompt, but there is one rule. Participants can only use one or two syllable words to discuss the topic. If they go over the syllable count, the referee stops them and says, "Stop, you are speaking incorrectly." The person then has to start at the beginning of the idea again and try to be understood.
>
> **Group Process:** After talking about how this felt to participants be sure to lead the discussion to what type of discourse is honored

and valued in the classroom. Ask participants to consider their own patterns of communication. Do they listen to all ideas? Do they talk over others? Are they reluctant to talk because they don't share the vocabulary or style of speaking as the dominant group?

Suggested Teaching Resources

- *Teaching for Change* (http://www.tfcbooks.org/best-recommended/slavery). This site also has many sources to help broaden all students' worldviews and support teachers in working towards inclusive anti-racist communities
- *The Zinn Education project* (http://zinnedproject.org/). For resources that would more accurately tell the story of slavery and resistance. The site offers numerous resources that disrupt multiple "single stories" regarding U.S. history.
- *Racial Equity Tools* (www.racialequitytools.org). This site provides extensive curricula, discussion guides, relevant data, an expansive glossary and more for individuals, groups, and institutions working towards racial justice.
- *Project Implicit Social Attitudes* (Implicit Association Tests; https://implicit.harvard.edu/implicit/). Students and teachers can log in and take an anonymous exam that helps reveal areas of bias that people may be unwilling or unable to acknowledge. This can be a helpful tool for educators working to be inclusive and to discover which attitudes and biases may be hindering one's progress.

References

Adichie, C. N. (2009, July). *Chimamanda Ngozi Adichie: The Danger of a Single Story* [Video file]. Retrieved from https://www.ted.com/talks/chimamanda_adichie_the_danger_of_a_single_story?language=en

Affolter, T. (2013). Piano lessons: A white teacher struggles to share the spotlight. In J. M. James, N. Peterson, & B. Christianson (Eds.), *White women getting real about race: Their stories about what they learned teaching in diverse classrooms* (pp. 101–114). Sterling, VA: Stylus.

Ahram, R., Fergus, E., & Noguera, P. (2011). Addressing racial/ethnic disproportionality in special education: Case studies of suburban districts. *Teachers College Record, 113*(10), 2233–2266.

Alexander, M. (2012). *The new Jim Crow: Mass incarceration in the age of colorblindness.* New York, NY: The New Press.

Alvarez, J. (2009). *Return to sender.* New York, NY: Alfred A. Knopf.

Anderson, D. (2006). Inclusion and interdependence: Students with special needs in the regular education classroom. *Journal of Education and Christian Belief, 10*(1), 43–59.

Annamma, S. A., Connor, D., & Ferri, B. (2013). Dis/ability critical race studies (DisCrit): Theorizing at the intersections of race and dis/ability. *Journal of Race, Ethnicity, and Education, 16*(1), 1–31.

Armstrong, T. (2000). *Multiple intelligences in the classroom.* Alexandria, VA: Association for Supervision and Curriculum Development.

Ayers, W. (2004). *Teaching the personal and the political: Essays on hope and justice.* New York, NY: Teachers College Press.

Baglieri, S., Bejoian, L., Broderick, A., Connor, D., & Valle, J. (2011). (Re)claiming "inclusive education" toward cohesion in educational reform:

Disability studies unravels the myth of the normal child. *Teachers College Record, 113*(10), 2122–2154.

Balcazar, F., Suarez-Balcazar, Y., Taylor-Ritzler, T., & Keys, C. B. (Eds.). (2010). *Race, culture and disability: Rehabilitation science and practice.* Sudbury, MA: Jones and Bartlett.

Baynton, D. C. (2001). Disability and the justification of inequality in American history. In *The new disability history American perspectives* (pp. 33–56). New York: New York University Press.

Beauboeuf-Lafontant, T. (1999). A movement against and beyond boundaries: "Politically relevant teaching" among African American teachers. *Teachers College Record, 100*(4), 702–723.

Bell, D. (1992). *Faces at the bottom of the well: The permanence of racism.* New York, NY: Basic Books.

Bernal Delgado, D., & Sleeter, C. (2005). Critical pedagogy, critical race theory, antiracist education: Implications for multicultural education. In N. Denzien & Y. Lincoln (Eds.), *The SAGE Handbook of Qualitative Research* (3rd ed., pp. 240–257). Thousand Oaks: SAGE.

Blanchett, W. J. (2006). Disproportionate representation of African American students in special education: Acknowledging the role of white privilege and racism. *Educational Researcher, 35*(6), 24–28. doi:10.3102/0013189x035006024

Blow, C. (2017, February 6). A lesson in black history. *New York Times,* p. A21.

Bourdieu, P. (1986). The forms of capital. In *The handbook of theory and research for the sociology of education* (pp. 241–258). New York, NY: Greenwood.

Burch, S. (Ed.). (2009). *Encyclopedia of American disability history* (Vol. 1). New York, NY: Facts on File.

Burch, S., & Joyner, H. (2007). *Unspeakable: The Story of Junius Wilson.* Chapel Hill: University of North Carolina Press.

Causton, J., & Tracy-Bronson, C. P. (2015). *The educator's handbook for inclusive school practices.* Baltimore, MD: Paul H. Brookes.

Cisneros, S. (1991). *The house on mango street.* New York, NY: Vintage Books.

Clare, E. (2017). *Brilliant imperfection: Grappling with cure.* Durham, NC: Duke University Press.

Coates, T. (2015). *Between the world and me.* New York, NY: Spiegel and Grau.

Cohen. R. (2016) School closures: A blunt instrument. *American Prospect: Longform.* Retrieved from http://prospect.org/article/school-closures-blunt-instrument-0

Connor, D. J., Ferri, B. A., & Annamma, S. A. (2016). *DisCrit: Disability studies and critical race theory in education.* New York, NY: Teachers College Press.

Crenshaw, K., Gotanda, N., Peller, G., & Thomas, K. (Eds.). (1995). *Critical race theory: The key writings that formed the movement.* New York, NY: New Press.

Dee, T., & Penner, E. (2016). The casual effects of cultural relevance: Evidence form an ethnic studies curriculum (CEPA working paper No. 16-01).

Stanford Center for Education Policy Analysis. Retrieved from cepa. stand-ford.edu/wp16-01

Delgado, R., & Stefancic, J. (Eds.). (2000). *Critical race theory: The cutting edge.* Philadelphia, PA: Temple University Press.

Delgado, R., & Stefancic, J. (2012). *Critical race theory: An introduction.* New York, NY: New York University Press.

Delpit, L. D. (2012). *"Multiplication is for white people": Raising expectations for other people's children.* New York, NY: New Press.

DiAngelo, R. (2011). White fragility. *International Journal of Critical Pedagogy, 3*(3), 54–70.

Dixson, A., & Rosseau, C. (2006). *Critical race theory: All god's children got a song.* New York, NY: Taylor & Francis.

Doig-Acuna, M. (2012). *Room for myself* [Unpublished poem]. Middlebury College, Middlebury, Vermont.

Donnellan, A. (1984). The criterion of the least dangerous assumption. *Behavioral Disorders, 9*, 141–150.

Donnor, J. K. (2005). Towards interest-convergence in the education of African-American football student athletes in major college sports. *Race Ethnicity and Education, 8*(1), 45–67.

Donnor, J. K. (2014). Education as the property of whites: African Americans' continued quest for good schools. In *Handbook of critical race theory in education* (1st ed., pp. 215–223). New York, NY: Routledge.

Douglass, F., & Foner, P. S. (1950). *The life and writings of Frederick Douglass.* New York, NY: International.

Du Bois, W. E. B. (1998). The souls of white folk. In D. R. Roediger (Ed.), *Black on white: Black writers on what it means to be white* (pp. 184–199). New York, NY: Schocken Books. (Original work published in 1920)

Emdin, C. (2016). *For white folks who teach in the hood . . . and the rest of y'all too: Reality pedagogy and urban education.* Boston, MA: Beacon.

Erevelles, N., & Minear, A. (2010). Unspeakable offenses: Untangling race and disability in discourses of intersectionality. *Journal of Literary & Cultural Disability Studies, 4*(2), 127–146.

Facing History and Ourselves. (2002). *Race and membership in American history: The eugenics movement.* Brookline, MA: Author.

Freire, P. (2018). *Pedagogy of the oppressed 50th anniversary edition.* (2018). New York, NY: Bloomsbury. (Originally published in 1970)

Ganeshram, R. (2016). *A birthday cake for George Washington.* New York, NY: Scholastic.

Gardiner, F., Diaz, M., & Brown, L. X. (2016, July 28). Charles Kinsey's story is about race. It's also about ableism. *Sojourners.* Retrieved from https://sojo.net/articles/charles-kinseys-story-about-race-its-also-about-ableism

Gillborn, D. (2005). Education policy as an act of white supremacy: Whiteness, critical race theory and education reform [Abstract]. *Journal of Education Policy, 20*(4), 485–505. doi:0.1080/02680930500132346

Goldring, R., Taie, S., & Riddles, M. (2014). Teacher attrition and mobility: Results from the 2012–13 teacher follow-up survey (NCES 2014-077). *US Department of Education.* Washington, DC: National Center for Educational Statistics. Retrieved from http://nces.ed.gov/pubsearch

Gotanda, N. (1995). A critique of our constitution is color-blind. In *Critical race theory: The key writings that formed the movement* (pp. 257–275). New York, NY: New Press.

Gravios, T. A., & Rosenfield, S. A. (2006). Impact of instructional consultation teams on the disproportionate referral and placement of student in special education. *Remedial and Special Education, 27*(1), 42–52.

Harrell, E. (February, 2014). *Crimes against persons with disabilities, 2009–2012— statistical* tables (pp. 1–23). Washington, DC: U.S. Department of Justice. Retrieved from https://www.bjs.gov/content/pub/pdf/capd0915st.pdf

Harris, A., Ovalle, D., & Rabin, C. (2016, July 21). Bullet that struck caregiver was meant to protect him, police union prez says. *Miami Herald.* Retrieved from https://www.miamiherald.com/news/local/crime/article 91160077.html

Harris, C. (1993). Whiteness as property. *Harvard Law Review, 106*(8), 1701–1791.

Health, Education, Labor, & Pensions Committee. (2014, February 12). Dangerous use of seclusion and retraints in school remains widespread and difficult to remedy: A review of ten cases. Washington, DC: U.S. Senate. Retrieved from https://www.help.senate.gov/imo/media/doc/Seclusion%20and%20Restraints%20Final%20Report.pdf

Henry, K. L. (2016). Discursive violence and economic entrenchment: Chartering the sacrifice of black educators in post-Katrina New Orleans. In T. Affolter & J. Donnor (Eds.) *The charter school solution: Distinguishing fact from rhetoric* (pp. 80–99). New York, NY: Routledge.

Hoffman, S. L. (2014). Zero benefit: Estimating the effect of zero tolerance discipline policies on racial policies on racial disparity in school discipline. *Educational Policy, 28*(1), 69–95.

Holpuch, A., & Barton, E. (2016, July 21). Florida police shoot black man lying down with arms in air. *The Guardian.* Retrieved from https://www.theguardian.com/us-news/2016/jul/21/florida-police-shoot-black-man-lying-down-with-arms-in-air

hooks, b. (2003). *Teaching community: A pedagogy of hope.* New York, NY: Routledge.

Hurston, Z. N. (1990). *Their eyes were watching God.* New York, NY: Perennial Library.

Jacobson, M. F. (2001). *Whiteness of a different color European immigrants and the alchemy of race.* Cambridge, MA: Harvard University Press.

Jefferson, T. (1984). *Jefferson writings: Notes on the state of Virginia.* New York, NY: The Library of America.

Johnson, K. (2016, June 9). Idaho town is rattled months after reports of a brutal assault. *New York Times.* Retrieved from https://www.nytimes.com/2016/06/10/us/idaho-town-is-rattled-months-after-reports-of-a-brutal-assault.html

Johnson, M. (2011). *Pym.* New York, NY: Spiegel & Grau.

Jorgensen, C. M., Schuh, M. C., & Nisbet, J. (2006). *The Inclusion facilitator's guide.* Baltimore, MD: Paul H. Brookes.

Kailin, J. (2002). *Anti-racist education: From theory to practice.* Lanham, MA: Rowman and Littlefield.

King, J., & Chandler, P. (2016). From non-racism to anti-racism in social studies teacher education: Social studies and racial pedagogical content knowledge. In A. Crowne & A. Cuneca (Eds.), *Rethinking social studies teacher education in the twenty-first century* (pp. 3–21). New York, NY: Springer International.

King, M. L. (1963). *Letter from a Birmingham jail.* Retrieved from https://www.africa.upenn.edu/Articles_Gen/Letter_Birmingham.html

King, M. L. (1964a). *The Nobel Peace Prize: Martin Luther King, Jr. acceptance speech.* Retrieved from https://www.nobelprize.org/prizes/peace/1964/king/26142-martin-luther-king-jr-acceptance-speech-1964/

King, M. L. (1964b). *Why we can't wait.* New York, NY: Harper & Row.

King, M. L. (1968). *Remaining awake through a great revolution.* Retrieved https://kinginstitute.stanford.edu/king-papers/publications/knock-midnight-inspiration-great-sermons-reverend-martin-luther-king-jr-10

Kuo, J. (1998). Excluded, segregated, and forgotten: A historical view of the discrimination of Chinese Americans in public schools. *Asian American Law Journal, 5*(181), 181–212.

Ladson-Billings, G. (1995). But that's just good teaching! The case for culturally relevant pedagogy. *Theory Into Practice, 34*(3), 159–165.

Ladson-Billings, G. (2004). Landing on the wrong note: The price we paid for brown. *Educational Researcher, 33*(7), 3–13.

Ladson-Billings, G. (2009). *The dreamkeepers: Successful teachers of African American children* (2nd ed.). San Francisco, CA: Jossey-Bass.

Ladson-Billings, G. (2014, Spring). Culturally relevant pedagogy 2.0: A.k.a. the remix. *Harvard Educational Review, 84*(1), 74–84.

Ladson-Billings, G., & Tate, W. (1995). Toward a critical race theory of education. *Teachers College Record, 97*(1), 47–68.

Lombardo, P. (n.d.). *Eugenic laws against race mixing.* Retrieved from http://www.eugenicsarchive.org/html/eugenics/essay7text.html

Leonardo, Z. (2002). The souls of white folk: Critical pedagogy, whiteness studies, and globalization discourse. *Race, Ethnicity and Education, 5*(1), 29–50.

Leonardo, Z. (2004). The color of supremacy: Beyond the discourse of "white privilege." *Educational Philosophy and Theory, 36*(2), 137–150.

Little, J. W. (1990). The persistence of privacy. *Teachers College Record, 91*(4), 509–536.

Loewen, J. W. (2006). *Sundown towns: A hidden dimension of American racism.* New York, NY: Simon & Schuster.

Loewen, J. W. (2010). *Teaching what really happened: How to avoid the tyranny of textbooks and get students excited about doing history.* New York, NY: Columbia University Teachers College Press.

Lynn, M., & Parker, L. (2006). Critical race studies in education: Examining a decade of research on U.S. schools. *The Urban Review, 38*(4), 257–290. doi:10.1007/s11256-006-0035-5

Matsuda, L., Lawrence, C., Delgado, R., & Crenshaw, K. (1993). *Words that wound: Critical race theory, assaultive speech and the First Amendment.* Boulder, CO: Westview.

McIntosh, P. (1989). White privilege: Unpacking the invisible knapsack. *Freedom Press,* (July/August), 10–12.

McIntyre, A. (1997). *Making meaning of whiteness: Exploring racial identity with white teachers.* Albany, NY: State University of New York Press.

Mehan, H. (1980). The competent student. *Anthropology and Education Quarterly, 11*(31), 131–152.

Miletich, S. (2011, February 16). No charges against Seattle officer who shot woodcarver. *Seattle Times.* Retrieved from https://www.seattletimes.com/seattle-news/no-charges-against-seattle-officer-who-shot-woodcarver/

Miller, M. (2016, May 25). White high school football players in Idaho charged with sexually assaulting black disabled teammate with a coat hanger. *Washington Post.* Retrieved from https://www.washingtonpost.com/news/morning-mix/wp/2016/05/25/white-high-school-football-players-in-idaho-charged-with-raping-black-disabled-teammate-with-a-coat-hanger/?utm_term=.f7b927df6fcb

Moody, J. (n.d.). *The Abeneki in Vermont, New Hampshire, New York, and Southern Quebec: A short chronology.* Retrieved from http://www.mtholyoke.edu/~bushey/classweb/Page 3.htm

Moraga, C., & Anzaldúa, G. (1983). *This bridge called my back: Writings by radical women of color.* New York, NY: Kitchen Table, Women of Color.

Moule, J. (2005). Implementing a social justice perspective in teacher education: Invisible burden on faculty of color. *Teacher Education Quarterly, 32*(4), 23–42.

Mukherjee, S. (2016). *The gene: An intimate history.* New York, NY: Scribner.

Newsom, B. D., & Bissonette-Lewey, J. (2012). Wabanaki resistance and healing: An exploration of the contemporary role of an eighteenth century bounty proclamation in an indigenous decolonization process. *Landscapes of Violence, 2*(1), Article 2.

Nieto, S. (2004). *Affirming diversity: The sociopolitical context of multicultural education.* New York, NY: Longman.

Oakes, J. (1985). *Keeping track: How schools structure inequality.* New Haven, CT: Yale University Press.

Omi, M., & Winant, H. (2015). *Racial formation in the United States.* New York, NY: Routledge.

Palmer, P. J. (1998). *The courage to teach: Exploring the inner landscape of a teacher's life.* San Francisco, CA: Jossey-Bass.

Paris, D. (2012). Culturally sustaining pedagogy: A needed change in stance, terminology, and practice. *Educational Researcher, 41*(3), 93–97. doi:10.3102/0013189x12441244

Paris, D., & Alim, H. S. (2014). What are we seeking to sustain through culturally sustaining pedagogy? A loving critique forward. *Harvard Educational Review, 84*(1), 85–100.

Paris, D., & Alim, H. S. (2017). *Culturally sustaining pedagogies: Teaching and learning for justice in a changing world.* New York, NY: Teachers College Press.

Parker, W. C. (2003). *Teaching democracy: Unity and diversity in public life.* New York, N.Y: Teachers College Press.

Perry, D., & Carter-Long, L. (March, 2016). *The Ruderman white paper on media coverage of law enforcement use of force and disability: A media study (2013–2015) and overview* (pp. 1–39). Boston, MA: United States, Ruderman Family Foundation.

Pollock, M. (2008). *Everyday antiracism getting real about race in school.* New York, NY: New Press.

Pratt, R. (1973). Official report of the nineteenth annual conference of charities and correction (1892). In *"The advantages of mingling Indians with Whites," Americanizing the American Indians: Writings by the "Friends of the Indian" 1880–1900* (pp. 260–271). Cambridge, MA: (Original work published 1892)

Reid, K., & Valle, J. (2004). The discursive practices of learning disability: Implications for instruction and parent-school relations. *Journal of Learning Disabilities, 37*(6), 490–499.

Rist, R. (1970). Student social class and teacher expectations: The self-fulfilling prophecy in ghetto education. *Harvard Educational Review, 40*, 411–451.

Roediger, D. R. (1998). *Black on white: Black writers on what it means to be white.* New York, NY: Schocken Books.

Sack, K., & Blinder, A. (2016, December 8). Heart-Rending testimony as Dylann Roof trial opens. *New York Times*, p. A1.

Sharp, G. (2004). Old "yellow peril" anti-Chinese propaganda. *Sociological Images.* Retrieved from https://thesocietypages.org/socimages/2014/06/20/old-yellow-peril-anti-chinese-posters/

Skiba, R. J., Michael, R. S., Nardo, A. C., & Peterson, R. L. (2002). The color of discipline: Sources of racial and gender disproportionality is school punishment. *The Urban Review, 34*(4), 317–342.

Skiba, R. J., Simmons, A. D., Ritter, S., Gibb, A. C., Karega Rausch, M., Cuadrado, J., & Chung, C. (2008). Achieving equity in special education: History, status, and current challenges. *Exceptional Children, 74*(3), 264–288.

Stester, M. C., & Stillwell, R. (2014). *Public high school four year on-time graduation and dropout rates: School Years 2010–2011 and 2011–2012* (No. NCES 2014-391). Washington, DC: U.S. Department of Education.

Swartz, E. (1992). Emancipatory narratives: Rewriting the master script in the school curriculum. *Journal of Negro Education, 61*(3), 341–355.

Tate, W. F. (1997). Critical race theory and education: History, theory, and implications. *Review of Research in Education, 22*, 195–247.

Tatum, B. D. (2008). *Can we talk about race?: And other conversations in an era of school resegregation*. Boston, MA: Beacon.

Theoharis, J. (2013). *The rebellious life of Mrs. Rosa Parks*. Boston, MA: Beacon.

United to End Genocide. (n.d.). *Atrocities Against Native Americans*. Retrieved from http://endgenocide.org/learn/past-genocides/native-americans/

U.S. Department of Education Office for Civil Rights. (2016, March). *Civil rights data collection data snapshot: School discipline* (Issue Brief No. 1). Retrieved from http://ocrdata.ed.gov/Downloads/CRDC-School-Discipline-Snapshot .pdf

Villa, R. A., & Thousand, J. S. (Eds.). (2005). *Creating an inclusive school* (2nd ed.). Alexandria, VA: Association for Supervision and Curriculum Development.

Walker, A. (2006). *We are the ones we have been waiting for: Inner light in a time of darkness*. New York, NY: New Press.

Weiss, R., & Gillis, J. (1999, June 27). Teams finish mapping human DNA. *Washington Post*, p. A1.

Wilson, A. (1988). *Joe Turner's come and gone: A play in two acts*. New York, NY: New American Library.

Wilson, A. (1997). The ground on which I stand. *Callaloo, 20*(3), 493–503. doi:10.1353/cal.1998.0096

Wilson, W. (1860/1998). What shall we do with the white people? In D. Roediger (Ed.), *Black on white: Black writers on what it means to be white* (pp. 58–66). New York, NY: Schocken Books.

Wise, T. J. (2005). *White like me*. Brooklyn, NY: Soft Skull Press.

Yosso, T. J. (2005). Whose culture has capital? A critical race theory discussion of community cultural wealth. *Race Ethnicity and Education, 8*(1), 69–91.

Zion, S., & Blanchett, W. (2011). [Re] conceptionalizing inclusion: Can critical race theory and interest convergence be utilized to achieve inclusion and equity for African American students? *Teachers College Record, 113*(10), 2186–2205.